making
kumihimo
japanese interlaced braids

Rodrick Owen

making
kumihimo
japanese interlaced braids

Rodrick Owen

GUILD OF
MASTER CRAFTSMAN
PUBLICATIONS

First published 2004 by

Guild of Master Craftsman Publications Ltd,
166 High Street, Lewes,
East Sussex BN7 1XU

Reprinted 2004

ISBN 1 86108 312 2
A catalogue record of this book is available from the British Library.

Publisher: Paul Richardson
Art Director: Ian Smith
Production Manager: Stuart Poole
Managing Editor: Gerrie Purcell
Commissioning Editor: April McCroskie
Editor: James Evans
Art Editor: Gilda Pacitti
Illustrators: John Yates and Simon Rodway
Photography (except where stated otherwise): Anthony Bailey

Typefaces: Garamond and Optima

Colour origination: Icon Reproduction, London, UK
Printed and bound: Kyodo Printing Co. Pte Ltd, Singapore

This book is dedicated to the memory of the late
Angela Lodge, and to her husband, Peter.

contents

part one:
before you start

part two:
the designs

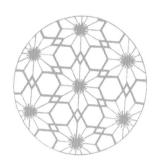

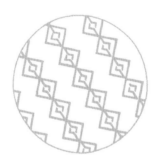

introduction

The takadai ('high stand') is a unique piece of kumihimo braiding equipment developed in Japan. It is not clear how or when the takadai came into existence. It was possibly developed from the braiding stands that are used by the nomads of Mongolia and ethnic minority groups in China. The takadai enables the braider not only to make flat braids that were once made by finger and loop manipulation, but also to make intricate double pick-up braids, which are more difficult to make in the hand.

At first glance, the frame of the takadai, with its warp threads organized and held under tension, appears similar to a weaving loom. However, there is a fundamental difference in the structure of what is made on each piece of equipment. Cloth woven on a loom is made with a vertical/horizontal structure, while braids made on a takadai have a diagonal structure known as oblique interlacing.

The vertical threads on a weaving loom are referred to as the warp. These are the threads that are held under tension and stay in a fixed position throughout the weaving process. A separate horizontal thread, called the weft, is cast by the weaver through a 'shed' (an opening) in the warp. It is a combination of how the warp and weft threads are worked together that gives the pattern variations found in cloth.

The warp threads for the takadai are arranged differently. Instead of being evenly spaced out as for weaving, the loose ends of one end of the warp are gathered, bound together and secured at the rear of the takadai. The loose threads at the other end are attached to bobbins and spread out diagonally over the arms on both sides of the frame. The warps pass between the pegs of carriers, called 'koma' (meaning 'horse saddle'), that rest in the grooves of the takadai arms. The koma keep the warps separated. The weighted bobbins hang free, creating tension on the threads.

Differences and Similarities

This book has been written for beginners, giving step-by-step instructions for setting up a warp and diagrams to complete the braids from each chapter. Most people who see a braider at work will associate the process with weaving. For instance, the action of opening the warp threads to create a shed and casting a thread through the shed looks to be the same as weaving. It was, therefore, decided to adopt weaving terms to describe the braiding process.

The takadai as it looks during the braiding process. The threads are attached to weighted bobbins in order to keep the braid under tension as it is made, and are kept separated by the pegs of the koma. Further details on the takadai and its associated equipment can be found on pages 24–7.

The words braid and plait have the same synonyms as the word weave; they all refer to the process of interlacing, regardless of whether it is made by hand or by using a piece of equipment.

As well as the alignment of the warp, a major difference between weaving and oblique interlacing is the weft thread. In woven structures the weft is an entirely separate thread from the warp, whereas in braiding the warp and weft are interchangeable – each warp thread takes its turn to become a weft in the process of braiding.

The second significant difference between weaving on a loom and braiding on a takadai is that created by the takadai's free-hanging bobbins. This unique feature allows for exciting structural possibilities, with the ability to use the takadai for three-dimensional structures. There are no harnesses, shafts or weaving-loom tie-ups to restrict or limit pattern choice. This is the takadai's unique and essential difference.

For some Western researchers who analyse different types of narrow fabrics, it is necessary to categorize and differentiate between structures in order for them to communicate with each other. Therefore, narrow fabrics that are generally known as braids have been divided into two groups. Those that are tablet woven and inkle-loom woven both have a vertical/horizontal structure and are called 'Bands'. While those narrow fabrics that are braided and plaited are known as 'Oblique Interlacing'. The Japanese, however, do not have such a clear-cut division; they group their vertical/horizontal 'ayatakedai' structures together with all their braids under one word: kumihimo (meaning 'gathering of threads'). Readers wishing to know more about the intricacies of structure should refer to books by Irene Emery and Noemi Spieser (see page 184 for a list of suggested further reading).

My interest in takadai is in its capacity to be used as a piece of equipment that has few boundaries. Adaptations to the equipment, like adding a pegged bar across the front of the frame, increase the possibility for structural experiment. Also, wider braids can be made by increasing the number of bobbins. There are two ways to do this: either by replacing the existing upper arms with longer ones, or by making koma with nine pegs. Many other adaptations may be possible.

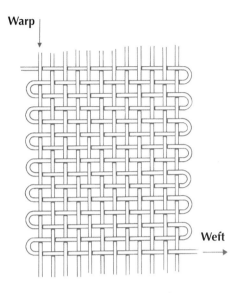

Above: 'Weaving' – cloth woven on a loom has fixed vertical warp threads with a separate weft that weaves horizontally through the warp threads.

Below: 'Braiding' – all the warp threads when set up on the takadai lay at an oblique angle. In place of a separate weft thread, each warp will take a turn to become a weft and interlace through the structure.

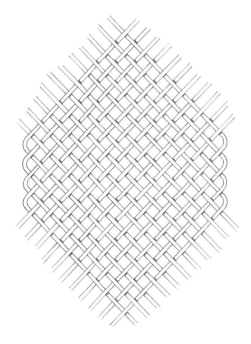

a kumihimo gallery

I do not see braids as only narrow strips, but as cloth on the bias. It was this view – shared by Warren Felton, an Idaho braider who has been making wide cloth for a long time – that led to the scarves seen on page 13. Other applications can be seen in the work of the various artists shown here. They use braids as functional and decorative embellishment for clothing, as jewellery, and for sculptural creations. The takadai encompasses both the simple and the complex, from basic plain weave with its focus on colour interactions, to complex pick-up braids with the emphasis on pattern.

Right: For Jennie Parry water is the essence of energy and life, and it inspires her sculptural forms. This piece reflects movement and power and is called 'Water Flow'. The twill double braids were alternately joined and separated at the edges to give the feeling of movement. They were made with 84 bobbins, each weighing 85 grams, using silk and linen fibres.

Below: This decorative textile from the collection of Gweneth Watkins is from North China. The small braids shown in this picture have been sewn onto a woman's collar, and it is not known exactly how they were made. They could have been made by loop manipulation or with loose ends on a Chinese coin braiding table.

Above: 'Jacket dedicated to the
memory of Denise Kavanagh' by
Heather Winslow. The wide braid
emphasizes the two sections of the
front and back yoke of this garment.
There are three different weave
structures in this jacket using variations
of four red colours. Additional details
include a square fused-glass button and
turned-back cuffs on the sleeves.

Above/Above left: The red, blue and green scarves were made by Richard Sutherland and the author using Zephyr – a 50% wool/silk yarn – at four ends per bobbin. The gold-coloured scarf made with 20/2 perle cotton is by Warren Felton. The scarves are approx. 6in (15cm) wide and were made in plain weave on the upper arm of the takadai with a nine-peg koma, using between 80 and 90 bobbins.

Left: Terry Flynn's vest is designed to highlight a wide silk braid made in multiple ends of silk. Because takadai braids are made on an oblique angle, they curve around necklines, creating many possibilities for collar and edge treatments. The main body of the vest is made of ultrasuede and features braided loop closures.

Left: 'Snow-shadows' jacket by Terry Flynn; braid made by author. A hand-woven shadow-weave pattern was chosen to suggest snowdrifts. The silk neck braid features a leaf pattern. In order to keep the pattern symmetrical, braiding was started from the centre out. Bobbins were re-attached and the remaining side braided.

Above right: For the 'frosted-leaf' choker, Terry Flynn used 8/2 reeled Chinese silk. The necklace was started with a braided loop and additional threads were inserted as the pattern was begun. The closure was created by working a Peruvian stitched bead around the ends of the top braid. The bead passed through the loop ending in a long draping tassel.

Below right: 'Twisted tassel – a bracelet with attitude' by Giovanna Imperia. The fine silk used to make this piece, hand-dyed Japanese silk organzine, has a high sheen, making the tassles soft and lively. The long tassels hanging down from the wrist flop open, giving them a life of their own as they move with the wearer's arm.

Right: 'Blue Moon' by Giovanna Imperia. This neckpiece expresses passions for tribal jewllery and is reminiscent of traditional ornaments worn by Rajastan men. It is a plain-weave braid split into three using metallic Japanese fibre, nickel wire, fabricated and oxidized sterling silver, and blue agates. The necklace is intended to be folded and twisted by the wearer.

Above left: 'Green Waves' by Giovanna Imperia. This bracelet is an open double braid that has been folded on itself and sawn to create a multitude of folds that can be opened or closed, thus changing its appearance. This specific design was developed as a way of simulating the folds of bracelets worn by, for instance, Middle Eastern women. The materials used are metallic fibre from Japan, nickel wire, and fabricated, etched and oxidized sterling-silver end caps.

Below left: 'Pods – Remembering Georgia O'Keeffe' by Giovanna Imperia. Made with a cross-over structure that creates folds or pockets resembling flower pods, this bracelet is reminicent of some of O'Keeffe's paintings – hence the name. This piece uses metallic fibre from Japan and nickel wire. The end cap is etched and oxidized sterling silver.

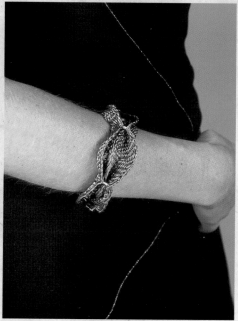

'If you have a lemon, make lemonade' scarf/sash by Giovanna Imperia. Materials: hand-dyed Japanese organzine silk, copper wire and glass beads. The warp was dyed in a range of yellows and chartreuse colours using a low-water immersion technique. This technique is not as controlled as warp painting, leading to many pleasant (or sometimes disappointing) surprises. In this case, the sunny yellow dye ended up dominating the other colours, making a very bright, striking warp, reminiscent of lemons. This brightness was further emphasized by adding brass-colour copper wire, which also creates an interesting three-dimensional piece.

part one:

before you start

interlaced braids: an overview

People have practised braiding skills for millennia, and while doing
so have developed multiple methods for making interlaced braids.
These include finger-braiding loops and loose ends, the bobbin-and-stand
methods, and ply-split twining.

The ancient and interconnected history of braiding is highlighted by the example of the mummies that were recently excavated in the Tarim Basin at Ürümchi in Western China.

Estonian woman working a braid from the outside edge to the centre. This is the same method of braid making as found in Japan and Palestine.

These show that the men and women who once lived there were about six feet tall, with light brown/red hair and Caucasian features. The sites also yielded many textiles, including the braids shown in the time line (see pages 19–22). In her book *The Mummies of Ürümchi*, Elizabeth Wayland Barber describes long lengths of braid sewn together to form a fabric that is dated 1000BC.

Did these early people bring their skills with them from the West and, if so, from which cultures? From a braiding point of view, similar structures exist in the Baltic States and the Eastern European countries stretching from the Baltic States down to the Black Sea. Long histories of braiding also exist throughout Asia, including Tibet, Mongolia, North-west India, and Uzbekistan.

Japanese Kumihimo

A major change in Japanese culture occurred with the arrival of Buddhism during the Asuka period (AD552–645). It is known that Chinese Buddhism had been embraced in Korea by the king of the Kudara (Paikche) kingdom, who in turn influenced the Japanese to adopt Buddhist practice. In Japan, Buddhism, supported by Prince Shotokutaishi, led to the building of the first Buddhist temple at Horyuji in Nara (AD607–615). Buddhists brought with them sutras and scrolls trimmed and tied with braids, and as the religion spread so did the need for braids. The Korean influence also extended to fashion – in the tomb of Takamatsu-Zuka near Nara, showmen and women dressed in Korean-style clothes with sashes tied loosely around the waist.

In Japan, as in most other parts of the world, braids were used in ritual and ceremony. For example, braids

In Japan, as in most other parts of the world, braids were used in ritual and ceremony

were used on various religious occasions as it was believed that God's presence could be found in the braid. They were also widely used by the aristocracy to decorate their clothing.

The evidence of Chinese and Korean influence in the use of braids by the Japanese might suggest that all the braids and braiding techniques originated in China or Korea, but this is not necessarily correct. Excavations of burial mounds from the Kofun period (AD300–500) yielded the Haniwa pottery figures (see time line, overleaf).

Earlier still, during the Jomon period (8000–300BC), there is evidence of textiles pressed into the clay to make patterns on the surface of the pottery. The word *Jomon* means 'rope pattern', and many of the impressions are made from twisted ropes or possibly braids.

In the Nara period (AD645–784), braids continued to be made and used for religious ceremonies. They were

a time line of kumihimo

1000BC

Excavations at the Tarim Basin at Ürümchi in Western China yielded many textiles, including these braids.

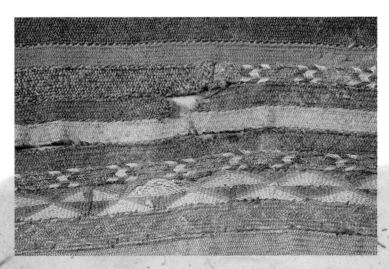

8000–300BC

Jomon period

Textiles were pressed into clay to make patterns on the surface of the pottery. The impressions on this pottery fragment appear to have been made from woven or twined threads.

also used to tie pendants, to secure mirrors and for Japanese *Musubi* (knot work). Evidence of such braids can be seen in the fragments that are preserved in the National Shoso-in Museum in Nara.

The Heian period (AD784–1184) saw Buddhism firmly established as the accepted religion, affecting all aspects of life. Temples contracted artists and craftsmen to produce work of beauty and quality, and this included braid makers. They developed two types of sophisticated and complex braids that were made by loop manipulation.

One group was a square, core-carrying braid that was made by the loop method using up to 144 strands (see opposite). They are called 'temple braids' after fragments found in hidden temple statues. The second form was a wide, supple braid called the Hirao sash, which was made with plied silk.

This design developed from the Chinese Sazanami chevron pattern, and became known as *Karakumi*. It was worn only by the emperor and high-ranking officials. The braid width varied from 6–10in (150–250mm) wide and was 8ft (2.5m) long. The outer edges are usually made up of a diamond design, while the centre panel is space-dyed and decorated with elaborate embroidery. The braid below (made by Kazuko Kinoshita) is a reproduction of a Karakumi design from the Asuka period (AD552–645). The original is one of the treasures of the Horyuji Temple in Nara.

The demand for flat interlaced braids surged during the Kamakura period (AD1185–1333) and continued through the Muromachi period (AD1333–1573). This was the time when the samurai warrior culture became powerful. Braids used in samurai

---

AD300–500
Kofun period
Haniwa pottery figures. The figures are dressed in ceremonial garments embellished with cords that are depicted as belts, garment closures and hair ties.

552–645
Asuka period
This braid is a reproduction of a Karakumi design from this time.

607–615
First Buddhist temple built at Horyuji in Nara.

armour were made by loop manipulation in 8ft (2.5m) lengths. About 800–1000ft (250–300m) of braid was needed to lace a suit of armour.

Sword-belt braids (*sageo*) were made to tie around the waist.

Samurai looked upon their sword as a sacred object in which the human spirit was embedded. Accordingly, great care was taken of both the sword and the sageo when the braid was hung up, because it represented that individual warrior's identity. As part of their training, samurai were expected to learn how to repair their kumihimo if it became damaged.

Towards the end of the Muromachi period, when peace came to Japan, the samurai influence shifted more to matters of state. Also, influenced by Zen Buddhism, they turned their attention to aesthetic pursuits like the tea ceremony.

A pattern favoured by samurai was this kikko design. Kikko, a hexagonal pattern based on the shell of the tortoise, is seen as a symbol of long life. The white braid that can be seen bound around the hilt of the sword serves to provide a good grip for the hand when holding the sword. (Instructions on how to make the kikko design can be found in the chapter on double braids, see page 116.)

As part of their training, samurai were expected to learn how to repair their kumihimo if it became damaged

---

645–784
Nara period

784–1184
Heian period
The square, core-carrying temple braid, below, was made by the loop method using up to 144 strands.

1185–1333
Kamakura period

1333–1573
Muromachi period
Braids such as the ones below are used to lace together the small metal plates that make up a samurai's suit of armour.

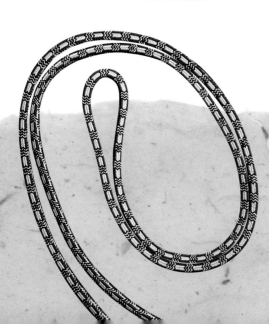

During the Monoyama period (AD1573–1614), the *Nagoya obi* became fashionable. This was a broad, round braid with tassels, which was tied at the back of the kimono. A narrow braid (an *obijima*) was tied over the obi to stop it from slipping. This was the beginning of braiding as it is most commonly known in Japan today.

The Edo period (AD1616–1867) and the Meiji period (AD1867–1912) were times of peace. The significant date of 1867 saw the start of great social change, when an order was issued that prevented the carrying of a sword in public. It was a time of mechanization; machines for making braids were introduced and the emphasis on braids changed from a masculine to a feminine use.

Prior to 1500, kumihimo was a luxury item that only the rich could afford. Its first uses as a belt for the *haori* half-coat are believed to have come from the *jin-haori* battle coats worn by military leaders. The modern upper-class women wore kumihimo belts. They were a status symbol that distinguished the aristocracy from common people. It was not until the late 1800s, when machines made these luxury braids, that they became available to women of all classes.

The period after 1945 saw the kimono replaced with a preference for Western clothes, which meant that braid makers were faced with change yet again. Books on how to make kumihimo began to appear and specialized schools were opened to teach the art of braiding. Today, kumihimo has also become popular in the West, and a whole different range of applications has been found for these beautiful braids.

1573–1614
Monoyama period

1616–1867
Edo period

1867
An order is issued that prevents the carrying of a sword in public.

1867–1912
Meiji period
Machines for making braids were introduced; the emphasis on braids changed and became a more feminine item.

Post-1945
Kumihimo has moved to the West with a whole different range of applications for these beautiful braids. The guitar strap below was made using silk yarn, with a silver buckle and ultrasuede end fittings.

the takadai

There are no known written documents to tell us how the modern-day takadai and the other three major pieces of kumihimo equipment were developed, or when they first appeared in their present form.

It is believed that the high takadai, as it is seen today, was designed to make braids to the maximum width of 68-bobbin pick-up braids that are used as an obijima. The equipment is balanced to position the braider so that all parts of the takadai are within comfortable reach, making for efficient use of effort and time.

Where did the idea for the takadai come from? Makiko Tada has suggested in her book on takadai braids that a prototype of the modern version existed around in Japan in the mid-1800s. This early frame may not have found favour, being less sophisticated than the modern takadai. Braiding, if it is the same as today, would have been practised as a family business, and in order for new technology to be embraced it had to prove more economical than the old technology.

The early frame would likely have been slower than loop braiding, and not so portable. It did not gain popularity, perhaps because of the resistance to changing directly from working with the hands to a bobbin-and-stand method. If the bobbin-and-stand method was about to be introduced, a question worth asking is where the idea was developed. Did the idea come from mainland China, or was it a Japanese idea? Whatever the answer turns out to be, the takadai is an amazing piece of engineering, simple in design, highly efficient and a joy to use.

equipment

To make the braids in this book you will need a takadai, bobbins and a few accessories. These are explained below.

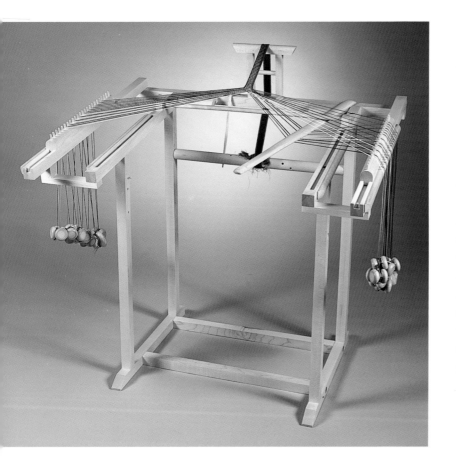

the takadai

The takadai can be purchased from one of the listed suppliers or can be made and assembled. The 'exploded' diagram opposite is for a slightly smaller version of the model pictured left.

The wood for the takadai should be a close-grained hard wood such as maple, sycamore or similar. It is important that when machining the slots for the koma in the inner and outer arms, there is sufficient clearance for the koma to run freely. Allow for any humidity changes that are likely to affect the wood causing it to expand. If this happens, the koma will probably stick. Details of suppliers can be found in the appendix on page 181.

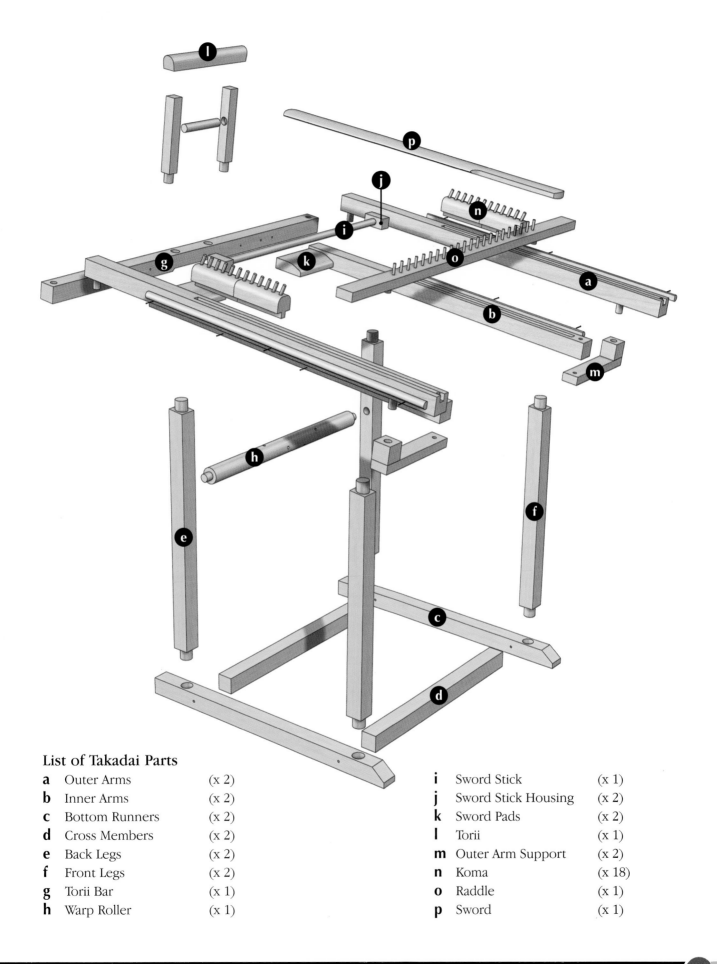

List of Takadai Parts

a	Outer Arms	(x 2)	**i**	Sword Stick	(x 1)
b	Inner Arms	(x 2)	**j**	Sword Stick Housing	(x 2)
c	Bottom Runners	(x 2)	**k**	Sword Pads	(x 2)
d	Cross Members	(x 2)	**l**	Torii	(x 1)
e	Back Legs	(x 2)	**m**	Outer Arm Support	(x 2)
f	Front Legs	(x 2)	**n**	Koma	(x 18)
g	Torii Bar	(x 1)	**o**	Raddle	(x 1)
h	Warp Roller	(x 1)	**p**	Sword	(x 1)

Bobbins

The takadai is constructed to make double braids using up to 68 bobbins. However, in the beginning it is not necessary to have that many bobbins. A good starting number is 40, as a good variety of braids can be made with this number and extra bobbins can easily be added later.

The Japanese name for bobbin is *tama*. Originally, bobbins were larger than those used today, and they were made from clay in a shape reminiscent of a Diablo or dumb-bell. Early bobbins were measured in a unit called a momme (one momme is equal to 3.75 grams). Today, bobbins are made from a close-grain wood with a metal insert to give the necessary weight.

The three bobbin weights generally available commercially in the UK and USA are 18 momme (70 grams), 23 momme (85 grams) and 27 momme (100 grams). Braids made in Japan for traditional applications are usually made with 100- to 110-gram bobbins, which produce a firm, rigid braid. 85-gram bobbins like the ones shown are more suitable for making flexible braids for Western applications.

Home-made bobbins

An inexpensive way to try out bobbins of different weights is to make your own using empty 35mm film canisters. The canisters are readily obtainable from shops that process and develop photographs, and can be filled with coins or metal washers.

Because the canisters have a smooth surface, they need to be covered so that the bobbin tie does not slip. Covering the outside surface with masking tape will give a good grip for the thread. To make the canister more like a bobbin another lid can be glued to the base of the canister. This will prevent the thread from slipping off.

Bobbin Ties

The tie is the link between the bobbin and the end of the warp. It acts as an extension to the warp, enabling a braid to be made to the full length of the warp and leaving sufficient loose ends for a tassel. Each bobbin will require a tie, and the instructions for making one are shown below.

Select and cut a strong fine-plied cotton yarn 39in (1m) long. Crochet cotton no. 20 or 30 is recommended.

Forming a bobbin tie.

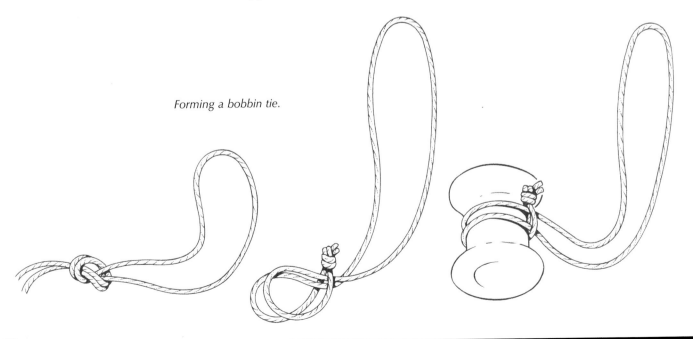

accessories

Several accessories are required. Their purpose is explained below:

Warping Posts or Frame

The posts or frame are used to measure out the length of the threads you will need to make a braid. The length that is measured is called a warp. If you are a weaver and have a warping frame (board), you will not need posts. It is important to remember that braiding warps are circular; they do not have a cross as for weaving. If you do not have a warping frame, all you need are warping posts and two clamps **(1)**, which are available from most weaving suppliers.

Freezer-bag Clips

Freezer-bag clips **(2)** have a vice-like grip that is exceptionally good for holding threads in position when setting up the braids, and for other applications during the braiding process. The use of the clamp will be described in the *setting-up* chapter (see page 44).

Flexible Clamp and Mirror

One end of the clamp is attached to the takadai frame; the other end holds a mirror **(3)**. The flexible hose is bent to position the mirror so that the surface of the lower double braid can be observed as you work. When making a double braid it is important to be able to keep a continuous check on the underside of the braid to see there are no errors.

Two-eyed Bodkin

This bodkin **(4)** allows you to start a braid with a straight edge. Details of how to set up the braid using a bodkin are given on page 40.

Odds and Ends

Other accessories include an 'S' hook, sales tags, size 20/30 Crochet cotton, and scissors **(5)**. The 'S' hook will be used when you start a braid with a loop. The sales tags are for recording information about samples made. The crochet cotton is used for all the wrapping and securing of threads during the making process, and at the end of the warp when the braid is finished off.

Magnetic Board

A magnetic board with magnets **(6)** will be needed when making double pick-up braids. It is an important tool that can be used to keep track of the pattern and thus reduce the possibility of making mistakes.

Rolling Pin

A rolling pin is used to roll down the length of braid once it has been completed, finished off and steamed. This flattens the braid and smoothes any bumps that might be present.

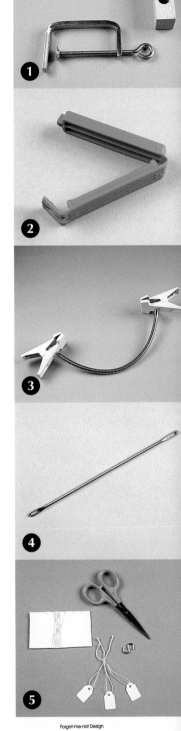

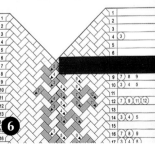

Forget-me-not Design

setting up

With the equipment assembled and the bobbins prepared, the next step
is to set up the takadai to make the first braid. This means selecting and
measuring the threads to be used, attaching them to the takadai and
winding the threads onto bobbins.

This chapter explains four different ways to begin a braid and five to finish one off. To summarize these methods: the beginning of a braid can be started with a tassel, a point, a loop, or with a straight edge. The braid can then be finished with a point, and secured by either twining or hemstitching. Alternatively, it can end with a tassel, a straight edge or the loose ends can simply be cut away.

Preparing to Set Up the Takadai
Before the threads are measured, thought needs to be given as to how the braid is to be started and finished. You should make this choice according to how the braid is to be used. For example, tassel ends could be the answer if the braid is to be a sash. If you are making a belt with a buckle, finishing will be simplified by starting with a straight edge.

Preparing the Warp
Measuring and cutting threads for a braid in weaving terms is called 'winding' or 'preparing' the warp. Thread is also referred to as 'yarn', depending on the texture of the fibre.

The width of the braid is determined by the number of bobbins, the thickness of the thread and the number of threads wound on each bobbin (referred to as threads per bobbin or ends per bobbin).

The length of the warp to be wound is calculated as the finished braid length plus an extra length that allows for take-up. Take-up is the extra warp that is used as the threads curve over and under one another. The angle of braiding also affects the take-up and may vary with each design made. As a guideline, allow 25% extra length for plain weave. For the first braids, cut the warp double the finished length and make a record of the before and after measurements on your record sheet. If you are planning an extra-long project or a large one using expensive fibres, it is well worth making a sample in order to determine more precisely how much extra warp is needed. All details such as this can be kept on the record sheet, a template for which can be found on page 180.

When the number of threads and the length is established, the warp can be prepared according to one of the four setting-up methods.

tasselled-end braid

Tassels are the universal way to begin and end a braid, adding drape and sensuality to a finished length however it is worn or used. Design 1 from the *plain and colour-and-weave pattern* chapter (see page 63) is used to explain the process of starting a braid with a tassel. The setting-up diagram (right) shows the set-up for the five-colour plain weave braid, a 25-bobbin braid with 13 bobbins on the right-hand side and 12 on the left. Coloured circles represent bobbins wound with thread.

The sequence of steps to prepare the warp and set up the takadai to make design 1 ready for braiding is shown below, explaining:

• winding and twining a warp
• tying off the tassel
• setting up the takadai
• attaching the bobbins to the warp
• making a weaver's knot and slipping hitch
• positioning the warp.

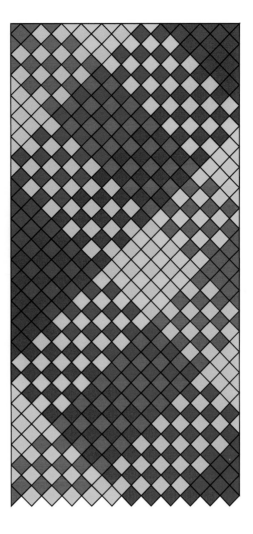

This coloured graph shows the finished braid pattern.

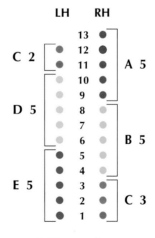

Setting-up diagram

NOTE
The five 'C' warp bobbins have been separated, two bobbins for the left-hand side and three for the right, and these are placed in separate positions on the warping posts.

Winding and Twining the Warp

1   If you do not have a weaver's warping frame, warping posts are an excellent alternative. They can easily be clamped to flat surfaces and adjusted to a given warp length. The posts can be used for warps up to 18ft (5.5m), and warps for takadai braids are usually no longer than 10ft (3m).

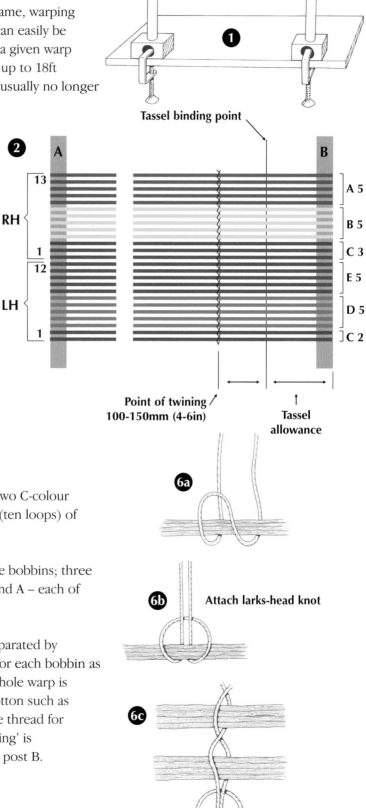

Tassel binding point

A 5

B 5

C 3

E 5

D 5

C 2

Point of twining /
100-150mm (4-6in)

Tassel allowance

2   Before winding the warp, calculate the number of threads for each bobbin. Set the warping posts to 39in (1m) and wind a continuous circular warp for each colour (there is no cross in the warp as for weaving). For this example, use four threads per bobbin (20 threads of each colour in total). Warp the left-hand side first, beginning with the two bobbins of colour C.

3   Tie the thread to post A and wind around post B. Begin counting the loops as you turn around post B. Two loops will equal the four threads for each bobbin.

4   After completing the four loops for the two C-colour bobbins, continue warping five bobbins (ten loops) of each of colours D and E.

5   Follow by warping for the right-hand-side bobbins; three of colour C (six loops), then colours B and A – each of ten loops.

Attach larks-head knot

6   The threads for each bobbin are kept separated by twining; that is, catching-in the threads for each bobbin as they are wound on the posts until the whole warp is secured. (Thin, strong, tightly twisted cotton such as Crochet Cotton Nos.20 or 30 is a suitable thread for twining and binding.) The 'point of twining' is approximately 4–6in (100–150mm) from post B.

Tying off the Tassel

1 Measure the tassel length and while the warp is under tension on the posts, compress the threads and bind the warp in two places approximately ³⁄₄in (20mm) apart.

2 Bind off the tassel tightly with a cotton cord. If the binding is loose, there is a danger of the warp threads pulling out of the binding when attaching the bobbins.

3 When the warp is finished and still on the posts, cut through the loops at both ends and place the warp to one side.

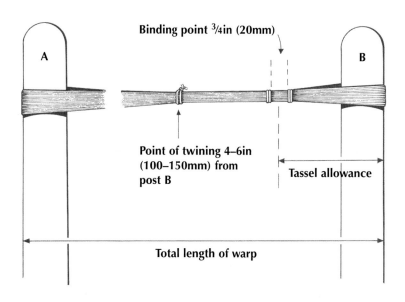

A

Binding point ³⁄₄in (20mm)

B

Point of twining 4–6in (100–150mm) from post B

Tassel allowance

Total length of warp

Setting up the Takadai

1 Bring the roller cord over the torii. Make a larks-head knot in the loop, insert the tassel, and tighten the larks-head to grip the braid between the tassel bindings.

2 Wind the roller towards you so that the cord lays evenly either side of the hole. Do not allow the roller cord to build up unevenly, as this will cause the braid to track off-centre as it comes over the torii.

3 Replace the brake (chopstick) and release the roller so that the brake leans back on the torii bar. The take-up for a quarter-turn of the roller is approx. ⁵⁄₈in (10mm), and ³⁄₄in (20mm) each half-turn.

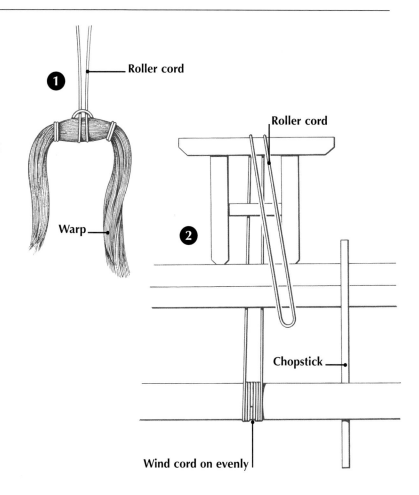

❶

Roller cord

Warp

Roller cord

❷

Chopstick

Wind cord on evenly

Attaching the Bobbins to the Warp

The next step is to attach and wind the warp onto the bobbins and arrange them on the upper arm of the takadai (the lower arms are used when making double braids).

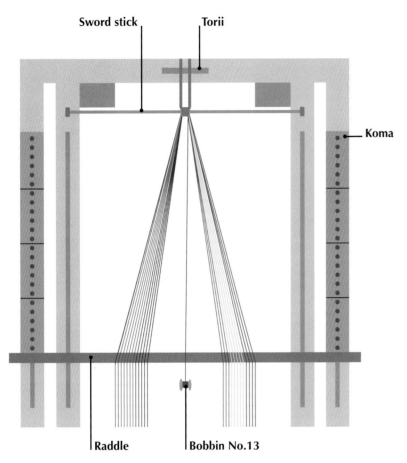

Sword stick   **Torii**

Koma

Raddle   **Bobbin No.13**

3 Separate the left- and the right-hand warps, and lay them over the raddle. Select from the right-hand warp the threads for bobbin No.13 and attach a bobbin, using a weaver's knot (as described opposite), and suspend it in the centre of the raddle.

4 Connecting the warp to the bobbin tie has to be completed while the warp is under tension. Keep the warp taut while pulling against the roller cord, and attach the bobbin.

5 The working length of the thread, from the tassel binding to the bobbin, should place the bobbins midway between the upper arm and the floor when the bobbin is suspended over the upper arm.

6 Bobbin No.13 will remain in this position at the centre of the raddle as a 'Marker Bobbin' for all the other bobbins to be measured against. It is important that all bobbins are the same length. Failure to ensure this will cause the bobbins to tangle while working.

7 Attach the bobbins to the remaining warp, working right- and left-hand warps alternately in descending numerical order, laying them over the raddle.

1 Place four koma on the upper arms with the pegs sloping towards the braider. Lay the braiding raddle across the upper arms of the takadai in front of the first koma.

2 Adjust the braid roller so that the larks-head knot is 6–7in (150–180mm) away from the torii. This will position the larks-head knot above and level with the sword stick. Insert the brake into the roller leaning back against the outer frame of the takadai.

Making a Weaver's Knot

1 Slip the loop of the bobbin tie onto the end of the warp, holding the bobbin tie in the left hand and the end of the warp in the right. Keep the warp threads under tension.

2 Fold the tail of the warp back over itself, making a loop, and pull the looped tail through the hole that has been made with the left hand.

3 Hold the loop in the left hand and pull down tightly onto the bobbin tie. The warp is now ready to wind onto the bobbin.

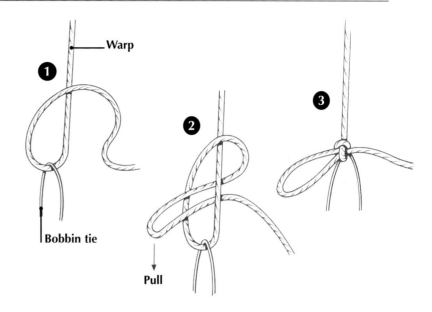

Making the Slipping Hitch

The warp should be kept taut while being wound onto the bobbin. Finish winding with the warp on the underside of the bobbin 33in (840mm) from the tassel binding.

1 Hold the bobbin in the left hand and place the thumb of the right hand under the warp.

2 Swing the bobbin away from the body, under the right hand, to form a loop, using the thumb on the right hand as an anchor.

3 Flip the right hand away from the body to the right to pull the slipping hitch onto the bobbin, pulling it tight against the warp on the bobbin.

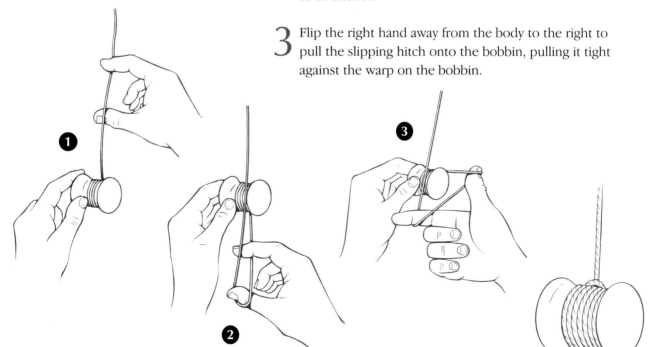

Positioning the Warp

1 The bobbins can now be transferred from the raddle and placed on the koma. Note that the top right-hand koma is left empty apart from the No.13 bobbin, which occupies the first bobbin space. The left-hand top koma remains empty.

2 Begin by placing bobbin No.13 in position. Then work down from the top, placing pairs of bobbins on the koma opposite each other. Bobbin No.1 will be placed in the first space on the second koma from the front.

3 Adjust the roller so that the 'point of braiding' is directly above the sword stick as you look down on the takadai. The position of the 'point of braiding' affects the tension of the braid, the higher towards the torii the steeper the angle of braiding.

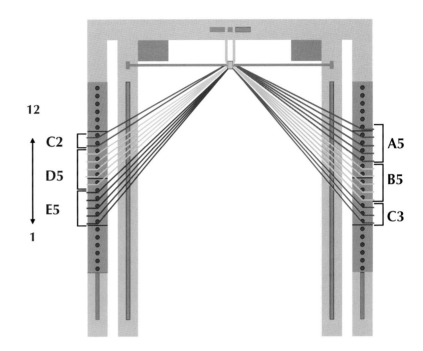

NOTE

The empty koma at the top is optional. The purpose of the empty koma is to create a sharper angle for braids of 25 bobbins or less. The sharper angle makes a tighter and narrower braid. Working without the empty koma will produce a looser, more flexible structure. In this case the No.13 bobbin on the right will be in the top bobbin position. The left-hand top bobbin position will be left empty.

Beginning Braiding

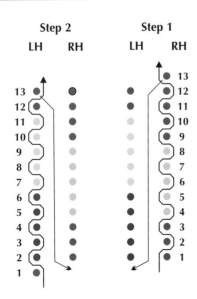

Braiding begins on the side that has the greater number of bobbins, normally the right-hand side. The 'how-to' instructions for making a braid are shown in diagram form. The diagrams give information about the colour and the positioning of the bobbins on the takadai arms, and how to weave your hand through the threads.

There are two steps to make this braid. Step 1 shows an undulating line, starting at bobbin No.1, moving under and over the bobbins to end at bobbin No.13. This is the pathway of the weave the right hand will make. The straight line from bobbin No.13 to below bobbin No.1 on the left-hand side shows the placement of bobbin No.13 when it is cast through the shed to the opposite arm. Step 2 is a mirror image of Step 1.

Making a Shed

The word shed is a weaving term given to the space that is opened up between the upper and lower threads. The hands are used to weave, not the sword. The right hand is used to create the shed on the right-hand side, and the left hand on the left-hand side.

1 For this plain-weave braid, the hand movements begin with the first thread lifted up on the back of the hand, the second thread is pressed down. The illustration shows the hand weaving through the threads to make a shed until bobbin No.12 is pressed down, leaving bobbin No.13 ready to be cast to the opposite side.

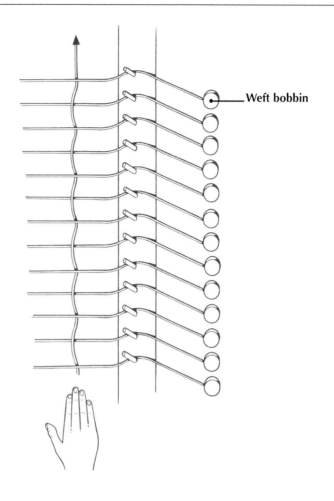

Weft bobbin

2 While holding the shed open with the hand, place the sword through the shed under the sword stick and onto the sword pad. This pushes down all the even-numbered bobbins, opening the shed. Leave the sword in position and cast the weft thread.

Casting a Weft Bobbin

1   Pick up the weft thread, casting it through the shed in one continuous flowing movement. Mastering this skill will require practice.

2   With the right hand, pick up the thread of bobbin No.13, lifting it vertically until it is clear of the koma. Swing the bobbin away from yourself in a pendulous motion and cast it through the shed. Finally, catch the bobbin with the left hand, while keeping hold of the thread in your right hand.

3   Keep the thread in your right hand under gentle tension and let it slip through your fingers while the left hand guides the weft. Place it smoothly into position on the left-hand arm.

4   On the left-hand side of the frame, use the left hand to pick up the bobbin thread and cast the weft. The right hand catches the bobbin before placing it on the right-hand arm.

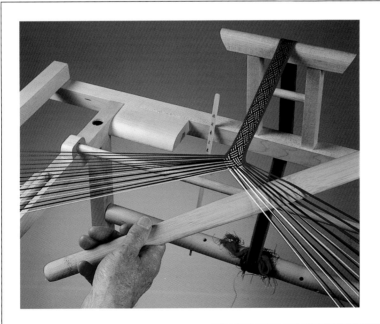

NOTE

Hold the handle of the sword loosely in the palm of the hand with the fingers touching one edge and the thumb on top. Pivot the sword between the thumb and the index finger using the remaining three fingers to push the handle against the ball of the thumb. Do not grip the sword tightly; the correct angle is better achieved with a flexible swivelling motion. This gives fluid control to the action of beating.

Beating the Warp

1 Once the weft is in place, the sword is released from the sword pad but left inside the shed ready to beat the weft into position. Use the sword in the right hand to beat the right-hand side of the braid. Likewise, use the left hand to beat the left-hand side of the braid. Beating firms up the weft from the previous cast, not the weft just thrown.

2 Beat with the middle part of the sword, keeping it parallel with the braiding line and slightly more towards the point of braiding (or *kensaki*).

NOTE
Never beat the edge of the braid, as this causes the edge stitches to distort and cram together. The pressure with which you beat should be preferably two or three short, soft strokes rather than one heavy wallop.

Working the Braid

This pattern is worked by continuously repeating steps 1 and 2 until the desired length has been made. After braiding six steps on both sides, the front koma will be filled with bobbins and will have to be replaced with an empty koma. To do this:

1 Lift the empty koma at the top of each arm (nearest the torii), slide the remaining koma up the arm and locate the empty koma in the front position (nearest the braider). This action is repeated every time six steps have been completed.

2 Next, check the position of the 'point of braiding' by winding the warp on to the roller, maintaining the point of braiding just above the sword stick.

Checking the length

It takes several six-step repeats for the braid to settle down and to establish a consistent width. At this point, insert into the side of the braid a glass-headed pin as a start point from which to measure. Pins can be inserted at regular intervals to give an approximate measurement as to the length so far completed. Note that the braids will be shorter when the bobbins are released.

Adjusting the Height of the Bobbins

As the braid grows in length the warp on the bobbins will shorten and will need adjusting. To do this, place the raddle across the front of the takadai, select the right-hand No.13 bobbin and place the thread over the raddle.

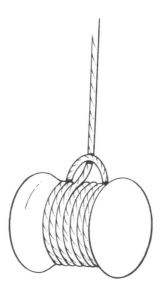

1 Release the slipping hitch (as shown left), letting the warp down to the required length, and then tighten the hitch by pulling the loop down onto the bobbin. Leave the bobbin suspended on the raddle as a marker.

2 Working down the right-hand side, bring one bobbin at a time to the raddle, adjust the height and return it to the koma. Repeat this process with the left-hand bobbins. Return the right-hand marker bobbin to the koma when all bobbins have been lengthened.

NOTE

At what tension should a braid be made? It all depends on what the braid is to be used for and what the braider prefers.

The tension is controlled by the weight of the bobbins used, how they are cast and placed on the opposite arm, and how the shed is beaten. Another factor that influences tension is the position of the point of braiding. The nearer to the torii, the firmer the braid is likely to be; the lower it is towards the braider, the looser the tension.

beginning with a straight edge

Braids started with a straight edge are useful as trims for garments, soft furnishings and small purses.

The warps for straight-edge braids are set up on a temporary pin, or, if the braid is intended to be an item such as a belt, it can be started directly on to the bar of a buckle. Both plain- and twill-weave braids can be made with a straight edge.

Plain Weave

This setting-up diagram (right) is for a three-coloured 25-bobbin plain-weave braid using 20/3 silk with four ends per bobbin. The large colour chart shows what the finished pattern will look like, and the diagram below shows the hand moves to make the braid. Note how the hand movements for this braid are different to those used to make the tassel-end braid (see page 29). This braid begins with the first bobbin pressed down, as opposed to lifting the first bobbin up.

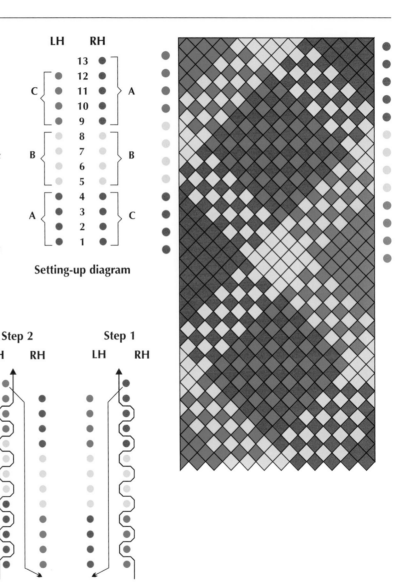

Setting-up diagram

Step 2   Step 1

Preparing a Temporary Pin

A bodkin with a double eye (see page 27) makes the ideal pin for straight-edge braids, as the holding cord can be threaded through the two eyes. (The bodkins are available by mail order, see page 181 for details).

   An alternative is to make your own, and there are many ways to do this. This pin (right) was made from a wire coat hanger. It was cut 4in (100mm) long, the indentations bent to shape, and the ends filed to remove burrs. The distance between the indentations is 2in (50mm). It is important to make the indentations shallow; just enough to secure the holding cord without it slipping. If the indentations are too deep it will be difficult to ease the finished braid off the pin.

Winding the Warp

1 Set the warping posts at 30in (750mm) apart and wind a circular warp counting four loops at post B as two bobbins. The warp for this braid will be folded in half over the pin, four ends for a right-hand bobbin and four for a left-hand bobbin.

2 Wind eight bobbins (four sets of four loops) for colours A, B, and C, plus an extra two loops of colour A. The extra two loops of colour A will be folded over the pin to give the four ends needed for bobbin No.13.

3 Cut the warp off at post A, keeping the colours separated.

The Holding Cord

Cut two 30in (750mm) lengths of strong cotton yarn, and thread each piece through an eye of the bodkin. Fold the two lengths in half, ensuring that the loops are level, and tie an overhand knot with the four loose ends. Make a larks-head knot with the roller cord, insert the holding cords and secure. Finally, wind the roller cord up until the pin is level with the sword stick.

Assembling the Warp to Pin

1 Place the raddle in position across the front of the takadai. Select the warp for bobbin Nos.7 right hand and 6 left hand (colour B), fold them in half and loop over the pin.

2 Cut two lengths of colour A and C as a security cord to match the colours on the edge of the braid, link them together and insert them through the assembled warp. When the braid is complete, the loose ends of the security cord can be sewn into the braid or discarded.

3 Clip the threads to prevent the warp from slipping, and attach bobbins. Place the bobbins over the raddle, letting them down to the correct height, and leave them in place as markers for the next pair.

4 Continue adding and interlacing pairs of warps in the sequence shown opposite. When all 24 bobbins are assembled on the raddle they can be moved to their respective koma positions.

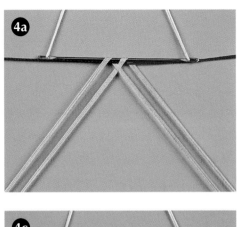

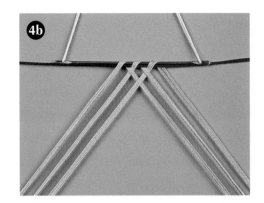

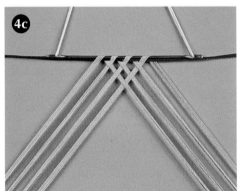

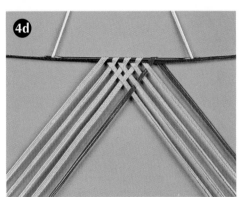

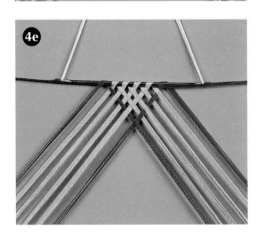

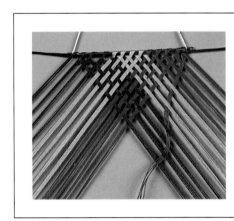

The Last Bobbin
The two 'A' threads are folded in half over the pin and tied to a bobbin. When all the bobbins have been attached, the braid is ready to work.

Making the Braid

Care has to be taken when starting braids on a pin not to hit the pin or the torii with the sword when beating. Attention has to be given to how the braid is bedding down, and the structure of the braid may have to be tightened and teased into position by hand. The completed straight edge can be seen here (right).

Follow the same procedure that was used to set up the plain-weave braid, copying the structure shown here.

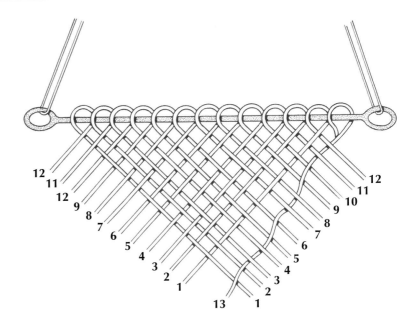

pointed end with holding cord

There are two ways to prepare a warp for a pointed end. The first (described below) is for a single braid. The second method is for single-coloured double braids, and is described later in the chapter on pick-up braids (see page 133).

This technique for starting braids is used by the tent dwellers in the Middle East, and is also found in pre-Hispanic Peruvian braids. A braid with a pointed end is excellent for belts. Although not all braid designs are suitable to be started by this method, it is particularly effective when using plain-weave or twill patterns, and for making wide braids.

This braid (right) shows the finished point with the loose ends of the holding cord. The loose ends can be sewn into the braid or stitched along the edge as a decorative finish when the braid is completed. This is shown in the section on finishing off (see page 48).

This 25-bobbin multicolour plain-weave braid was made with four ends of 30/3 silk per bobbin, using the hand moves from design 1. The setting-up diagram shows how the five colours will be arranged on the upper arms of the takadai.

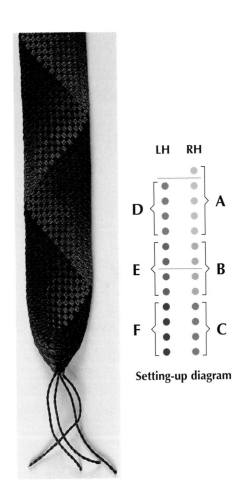

Setting-up diagram

Preparing the Warp

Set the warping posts 30in (750mm) apart ready to wind the warp. Start and finish at post A, and wind a circular warp for each colour counting two loops at post B as one bobbin.

Wind five bobbins of colour A and four each of B, C, D, and F. Cut the warps at post A, but do not cut the loops at post B. Keep the colours separated and set them aside.

Permanent Holding Cord

1 Choose a yarn for the holding cord that is strong enough to support the 25 bobbins. The yarn used in this example is the same as the warp threads – a tightly twisted silk thread. Use the same yarn as the warp (or similar), cutting two 30in (750mm) lengths of yarn.

2 Fold the two lengths in half, ensuring that the loops are even, and tie an overhand knot with the four loose ends. Make a larks-head knot with the roller cord, insert the holding cord and secure.

3 Wind on the braid roller until the loops of the holding cord are level with the top of the first koma on the upper arm, and secure the roller with the brake.

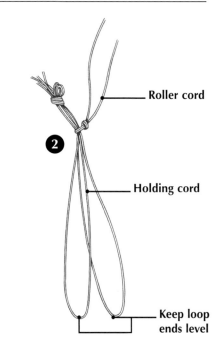

Roller cord

2

Holding cord

Keep loop ends level

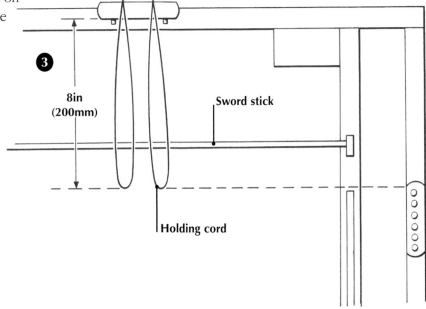

3

8in (200mm)

Sword stick

Holding cord

1 **Assembling the Warp** Place the raddle in position across the front of the takadai. Begin with the No.1 bobbin, selecting two cut lengths of colour F for the left-hand side and colour C for the right-hand side. Fold each colour in half, linking them together to make four ends per bobbin.

2 **Adding Bobbin No.1** Insert the linked colours into the loops of the holding cord. Pull the eight warp ends towards you, making sure that they are all the same length. To prevent the warp moving while attaching the bobbins, use the freezer-bag clip to secure the holding cord and warp. The clip is used each time warp threads are added. Adjust the height of the bobbins and leave them suspended over the raddle as marker bobbins. Remove the clip and set aside.

3 **Adding Bobbin No.2** Select and link the warps for No.2 bobbins, colours F and C. Before the threads for these two bobbins can be added the holding cord has to be twined. Twining secures the warps and strengthens the holding cords. The left-hand pair twine together in a clockwise direction ('Z' twist), and the right-hand cords twine counterclockwise ('S' twist).

    The lower cords come up on the outside of the upper cords, as the upper cords pass down between the lower cords. Visually the twining appears like a series of inverted Vs.

4 **Moving to the Raddle** Insert the warps into the twined structure, attach bobbins and lay them over the raddle on the inside of the No.1 bobbins. Move the No.1 bobbins from the raddle into position on the koma. The No.2 bobbins are now the marker bobbins for the No.3 bobbins. Continue attaching the warp to the holding cord until bobbin No.13 is ready to be attached.

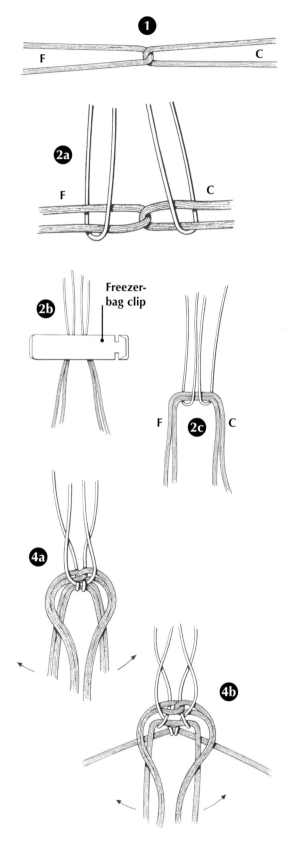

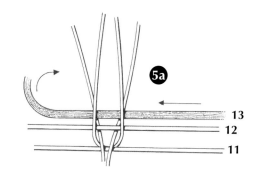

5 **Attaching Bobbin No.13** Select the warp for bobbin No.13 insert it from the right-hand side and lay it in on top of the No.12 warp. Twine the holding cord and bring the thread back through holding cords as shown in **(5b)**. Attach the four ends to a bobbin, and measure the length against bobbins No.12 on the raddle.

Move bobbins No.12 and No.13 from the raddle and place in position on the upper arm. The left-hand No.13 koma position is left empty.

Setting up is now complete and the warp is ready to braid.

NOTE
The first six passes of the weft when passed through the shed will lie vertical to the twining. Beat the warp vertically to snug it down next to the holding cord, and from then on beat at the normal angle.

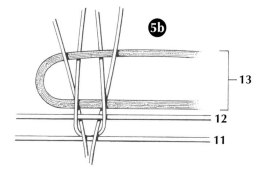

starting with a braided loop

Braids with loops are used to link and attach. In Japan, loops link to the kimono as closures. In countries such as in Peru, Tibet and India, loops at the end of slingshots link to the finger. Loops are also used as fasteners to capture buttons and as links at the end of belts and chatelaines.

Making a Loop on the Marudai

There are many eight- and sixteen-strand braid patterns that can be used to make the loop. The example shown (right) is for an eight-strand hollow braid using two ends of 30/3 silk yarn per bobbin.

Winding the Warps

Marudai Warp To prepare the warp for the loop, set the posts at 21in (530mm). Wind eight lengths of yarn counting eight loops at post B. Before cutting off the warp at post A, loosely secure the warp at post B with a larks-head knot and set the warp aside.

Takadai Warp Wind off the takadai warp counting 17 loops at post B. Loosely secure the warp at post B with a larks-head knot, cut the warp off at post A and set aside.

A single-coloured 25-bobbin braid with a loop. The loop is made on the marudai using eight bobbins, and then removed to have additional warp threads attached, ready for setting up on the takadai. The sequence of steps to make this 9in (225mm) braid are given overleaf.

Making the Braided Loop

1 Place the larks-head knot at the midpoint of the warp. As we are making a loop 1½in (40mm) long, we will offset the double binding from the midpoint to 'Z' by this amount, and tie a double binding at 'X' and 'Z'.

2 Remove the larks-head knot and feed the shorter length of the warp down through the centre hole of the marudai. Insert a double-pointed knitting needle between the bindings and attach one strand of silk to each of the eight bobbins.

3 Attach a counterbalance weight that is slightly less than 50% of the total bobbin weight to the warp on the underside of the marudai.

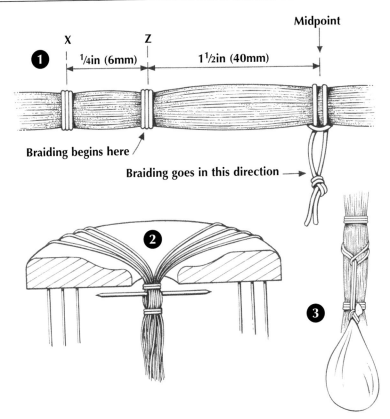

Midpoint

X   Z

1 ¼in (6mm) 1½in (40mm)

Braiding begins here

Braiding goes in this direction →

2

3

Braiding the Loop

1 Before you begin to make this braid, space the bobbins equally around the marudai as shown in Figure **(1)** (right) and remove the knitting needle. The braid is made by continuously repeating steps 1 and 2. While making this braid, 'drop' the bobbin into the new position. This helps give it a rounder, tighter finish.

2 Work the braid until it measures 1½in (40mm). Firmly tie off the point of braiding on the underside of the marudai top to prevent the braid from undoing as the bobbins are released.

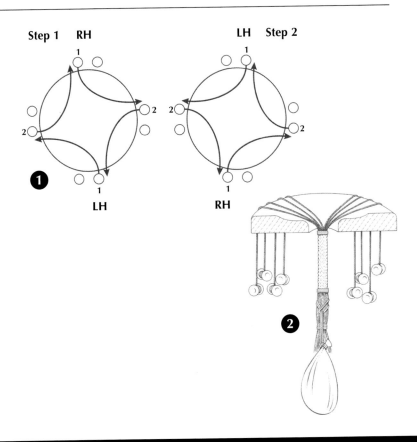

Step 1 RH

LH Step 2

1

LH

RH

2

Securing and Forming the Loop

1 Thread a needle with 24in (600mm) of thread that is the same colour as the warp. Slide the bindings down the warp a little way so the end of the braiding can be seen, and bring the two braided ends together to form a loop.

2 Starting on the right-hand side, sew through the braid from the front to the back. Bring the needle to the front of the left-hand side and sew through to the back, as shown. Remove the needle and make sure that both ends of the thread are the same length.

3 Pull the two sides of the loop firmly together. Hold the right-hand thread down at the front of the loop and wrap the left-hand thread tightly twice around both legs, working away from the loop. Half hitch the third wrapping at the rear of the loop.

4 Thread the ends of the yarn through the loop in opposite directions, tying a square knot between the legs of the loop to secure the wrapping.

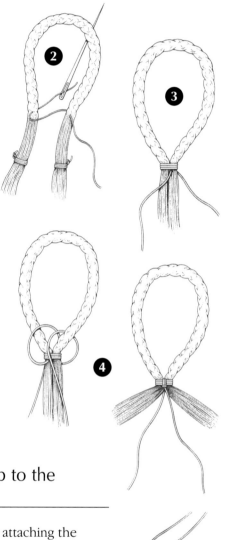

Adding the Takadai Warp

Centre the takadai warp that was set aside, place it between the legs of the braided loop and secure the warp to the loop with a square knot. The warp is now ready to be set up on the takadai. Later, when the braid is complete, sew the loose ends into the braid.

Attach the Warp to the Roller Cord

The final step before attaching the bobbins to the takadai warp is to secure the warp to the roller cord. To prevent any stress on the braided loop, use a thin, strong cotton yarn.

Cut a 8in (200mm) length of yarn and thread it through the loop. Bring the two ends together and tie an overhand knot about 3in (75mm) away from the loop (as shown, right). Make a larks-head knot in the roller cord, insert the overhand knot and pull tight.

Attaching the Bobbins

1 Place the raddle in position at the front of the takadai. Begin with the braided loop warp as this is securely anchored by the wrapping. This warp will allocate to koma positions 10–13 on the right and 9–12 on the left.

2 Select the right-hand loop warp and remove the binding. Attach two ends of warp to each of the four bobbins and suspend them over the raddle. Repeat this for the left-hand side.

3 Leave right-hand No.10 bobbin on the raddle as a marker bobbin and place the remaining bobbins on the upper arms as shown in the setting-up diagram.

4 Attach bobbins to the takadai warp alternating between sides and place them over the raddle. When complete place them on the upper arms.

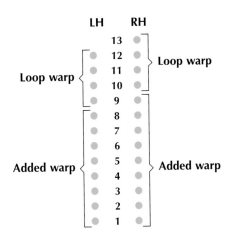

Setting-up diagram

Making the Braid

This 25-bobbin braid is made in a four-step repeating sequence. Steps 1–4 are 2/2 twill; steps 5–8 are plain weave. Begin making a length of twill-weave braid, before starting the eight-step sequence shown below.

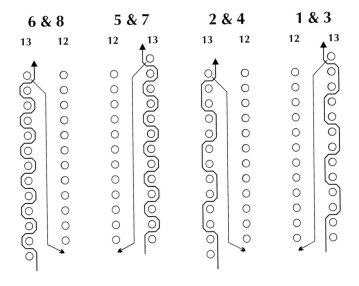

finishing off the braid

No matter what technique is used to start the braid, all braids finish up with loose ends that need to be secured to stop the braid unravelling. A 25-bobbin braid is used to explain five finishes. Four techniques show different ways of finishing with tassels, while the fifth shows how to cut away the loose ends completely, leaving a clean edge.

Releasing the Bobbins

Whichever technique is used to finish off the braid, the final act will be to release the bobbins from the warp.

Begin by removing the warp from bobbins No.1 and 2 on both sides of the takadai. This takes the tension away from the point of braiding. Continue removing the higher number bobbins, working down the warp until all the bobbins are released.

Wrapped Tassels

Tying off the end of a braid to secure the loose ends is the method most commonly associated with braid endings. This must be done in such a way that it does not pull off the end of the braid.

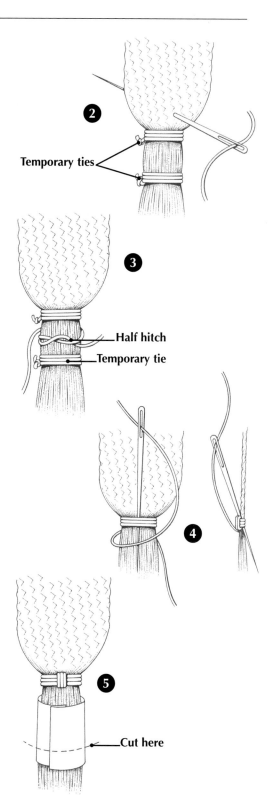

Temporary ties

Half hitch
Temporary tie

Cut here

1. Tightly secure the loose threads at the end of the finished braid with a temporary tie, and remove the warp from the takadai. Leave the temporary ties in position until the permanent wrapped finish has been completed.

2. Cut a length of thread using one of the warp colours and thread onto a needle. Gather and pinch together all the warp threads above the temporary tie. Sew through the braid at an angle and let one end fall down, joining the loose ends.

3. Remove the thread from the needle and, working towards the tassel, wrap three turns firmly around the braid, finishing off with a half hitch.

4. Re-thread the needle and stitch as follows: stitch over and back under the wrapping two times, working towards the tassel. On the third pass, sew through the braid to below the wrapping on the opposite side. Repeat on the other side and let the remaining loose thread fall down as part of the tassel.

5. To finish off the tassel with neat, straight ends, remove the temporary tie and wrap the loose ends tightly in a thin strip of paper. Cut through the paper with the throat of the scissors.

Pointed End

Braids ending with a point can be finished by either twining or by hemstitching. This is always carried out while the braid is still on the takadai and held under tension.

Twining

Begin by anchoring a pair of twining threads into the braid structure, and start twining the right-hand side. Work down from the edge to the centre of the braid. Twine (twist) the two threads firmly in a counterclockwise direction, catching in the threads of each bobbin. Continue to twine around the point of braid and up to the No.12 bobbin on the left-hand side. Sew the loose ends into the braid and secure them.

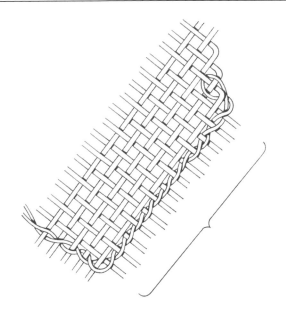

Hemstitching

1 Choose a fine yarn and thread a needle ready for hemstitching. Begin by anchoring the yarn into the braid structure on the right-hand side of the braid. Slide the needle under warps 12 and 13.

2 Bring the needle back over warp threads 12 and 13, and insert it diagonally under the braid into the braid structure two rows in, between bobbin Nos.11 and 12. Pull the stitch firm, but not tight.

3 Bring the needle down, inserting it between warp threads 11 and 12, and stitch under bobbin Nos.10 and 11. Repeat steps 1 and 2, working down the right-hand side and back up the left-hand side. Secure the loose ends in the braid when hemming is completed.

The hemstitch turns around the point of the braid.

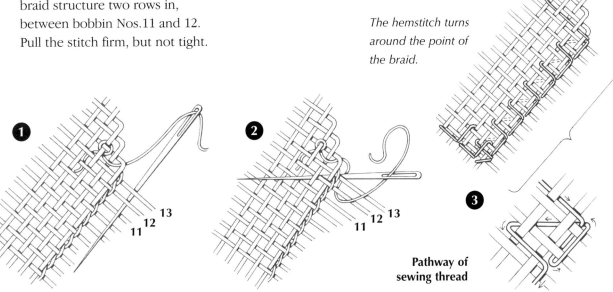

Pathway of sewing thread

Releasing the Warp

When the braid is finished and secured, release the bobbins from the warp.

1 Start with bobbin Nos.1 and 2 on both sides of the braid; this takes the tension off the point. Then work down from bobbin Nos.12 and 13, alternating sides until all the remaining bobbins are released.

2 To twine or hemstitch the beginning of the braid in order to match the completed ending, lay the braid on a cushion with the front of the braid facing up. Identify the pathway of the pattern, hold the braid under tension, and attach the working threads to the edge of the braid. Hemstitch or twine diagonally down to the point and back up the other side, and then stitch the sewing thread into the braid to secure them. Use two needles, alternating them to twine the edge.

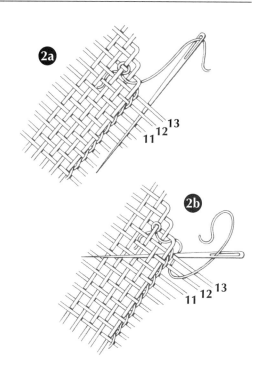

Finishing with a Straight Edge

1 To create a straight edge, the bobbins that make the pointed end have to be converted from their active role to a passive one. To do this, stop braiding when there are 13 bobbins on the right-hand upper arm and add four koma to each of the lower arms. It takes 12 steps to change all 25 bobbins to a passive role (see the chart overleaf). Each step transfers bobbins from the upper to the lower arms, taking them out of the active warp. The transfer is carried out in two ways: by lifting the bobbins marked 'A' and placing them onto the lower arm, or by casting the bobbins marked 'B' through the warp to the lower arm. Note: in step 2 there is only one bobbin move.

2 When all the steps are complete, place the raddle across the front of the takadai. Transfer all the bobbins, keeping them in the same order, from the lower arm to the raddle, ready for twining.

3 Cut a length of one of the warp yarns, fold it in half, and catch the loop around the left-hand warp thread. Twine across the braid tight up to the finished warp following the illustration. Secure the loose ends by sewing them into the braid.

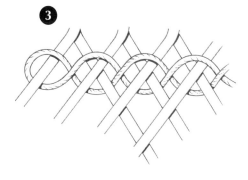

Here, a white thread has been used to illustrate the horizontal twining.

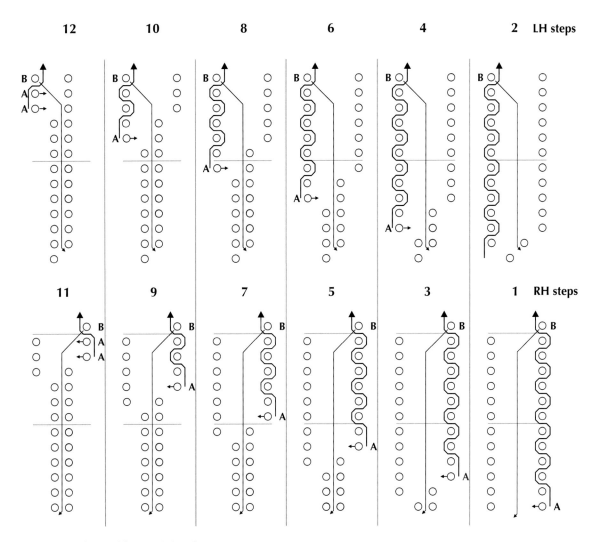

12	10	8	6	4	2	LH steps

11	9	7	5	3	1	RH steps

Instructions for finishing with a straight edge

A BRAID WITHOUT TASSELS

When making a length of braid for a belt or a guitar strap, both ends need to be totally free of tassels. Starting a braid with a point or straight edge is a possible answer for one end, but that still leaves the loose warp threads at end of the braid. The instructions opposite show one way to remove the loose ends and leave the end of the braid with a straight edge.

Cutting the Braid

1 Make the braid a little longer than the required finished length, secure the warp and remove from the takadai. Measure from the beginning of the braid and mark the finished length. Use a sewing machine and straight stitch across the braid width several times, making sure to catch in the threads on the edges of the braid.

2 Just below the stitching, apply 'Fray Check' or a similar product across both sides and the edges of the braid. This will hold the braid structure together and stop it unravelling. Let the solution dry and cut through the sealed area with a sharp knife, removing the unwanted braid and tassel.

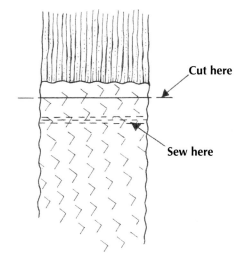

Cut here

Sew here

Creating the Envelope

The next step is to cover the cut end with an envelope of fabric. Use a piece of fabric that has been cut on the bias, and follow these four steps.

1 To work out the exact size of the bias cloth needed, make and fold a paper sample over the braid. Place the cloth on the front of the braid and stitch it onto the braid.

2 Fold the fabric back on itself so that it lies under and above the braid.

3 Then fold the sides into the centre of the braid.

4 Make a horizontal fold and pull the flap down onto the braid. Secure this with a pin and stitch the sides and edges of the envelope to the braid.

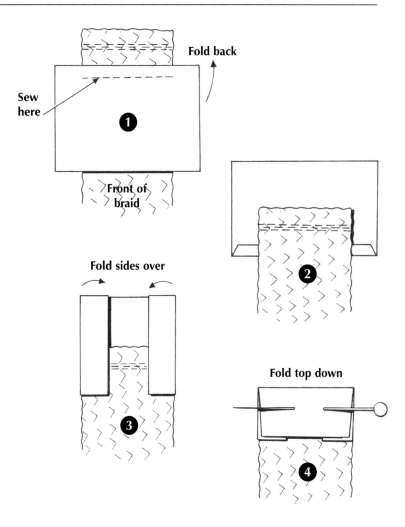

creating your own designs

There will come a time when you will wish to make a braid that varies from the standard Japanese braid designs. It could be to change the pattern, colour or the width of the braid. To do this you will need to construct a graph.

Follow the instructions set out below and construct a graph for your own design by adapting one of the master graphs in the appendix (see page 160). These instructions apply whether using a computer or working with pencil and paper. The computer graphics in this book were created using CorelDraw. This programme, like others of its type, makes it possible not only to create a graph, but also to colour a pattern by 'clicking' into the spaces in the grid.

Creating a Graph for Plain Weave
Working with an odd number of bobbins The stitches of the plain weave structure are represented on a graph as full and half-diamond shapes. The width of odd-numbered plain-weave braids increases in four bobbin increments. For every four bobbins added the number of diamond spaces on the graph between the right-hand and left-hand edges increases by two spaces. Always read the graph from the right-hand side as shown in the chart and setting up diagram below. Also, see Rule 1 (below right).

Plain weave graph widths for odd bobbin braids. The graph reads from left to right

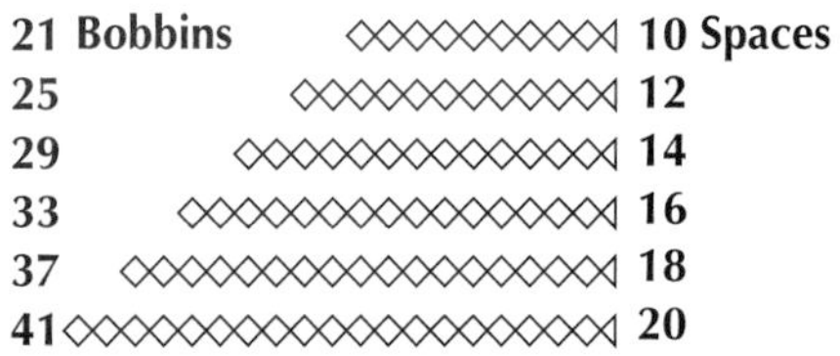

21 Bobbins	⟨⟩⟨⟩⟨⟩⟨⟩⟨⟩	10 Spaces
25	⟨⟩⟨⟩⟨⟩⟨⟩⟨⟩⟨⟩	12
29	⟨⟩⟨⟩⟨⟩⟨⟩⟨⟩⟨⟩⟨⟩	14
33	⟨⟩⟨⟩⟨⟩⟨⟩⟨⟩⟨⟩⟨⟩⟨⟩	16
37	⟨⟩⟨⟩⟨⟩⟨⟩⟨⟩⟨⟩⟨⟩⟨⟩⟨⟩	18
41	⟨⟩⟨⟩⟨⟩⟨⟩⟨⟩⟨⟩⟨⟩⟨⟩⟨⟩⟨⟩	20

Note: whole and half-diamonds = one space

Drawing a graph

Work through the procedure below to prepare and colour a graph for a three-coloured, 21-bobbin log-cabin design.

From the Appendix, copy a page of Fig A01 (page 161). Draw a vertical line down the page to define the right-hand side of the braid. Refer to the graph below left and apply Rule 1, counting nine and a half diamond spaces across the graph, starting with a half diamond, and draw the left-hand edge of the braid. The horizontal rows of diamonds on the graph should at least equal the total number of bobbins.

Colouring the pattern

1 Transfer the three-colour setting-up diagram below to the graph. Line up the bobbins level with the half-diamonds on the graph, making sure that the left-hand bobbin No.12 starts one row down from bobbin No.13 on the right-hand edge. Odd-numbered braids are asymmetrical; the patterns always appearing slightly off-centre.

2 To show the placement of the left-hand stitches as they reach the right-hand side of the graph, add the left-hand bobbins below the right-hand bobbins in one continuous line and colour in the edge stitches (see illustration **(2)** on facing page).

Before colouring in the pattern note how the stitches turn at the edge of the braid. Figure **(3)** shows both the correct and incorrect pathway to plot stitches on the graph.

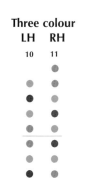

Three colour
LH   RH
10   11

Setting-up diagram

RULE 1:

Graphs for an odd number of bobbins always read from the right-hand side. The number of diamond spaces between the vertical edges of the braid is always equal to the left-hand bobbin count in the setting-up diagram.

2 Read graph left to right

3

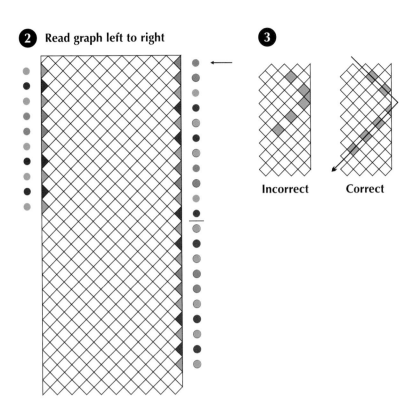

Incorrect   Correct

NOTE
A common mistake is to turn the stitch immediately it hits the edge of the graph. The 'correct' way shows how the stitch has to go under a stitch on the edge before descending in the opposite diagonal.

3   Colour in the pattern working first from the right-hand side down to the left-hand side and then work down from the left-hand side to the right **(4)** and **(5)**.

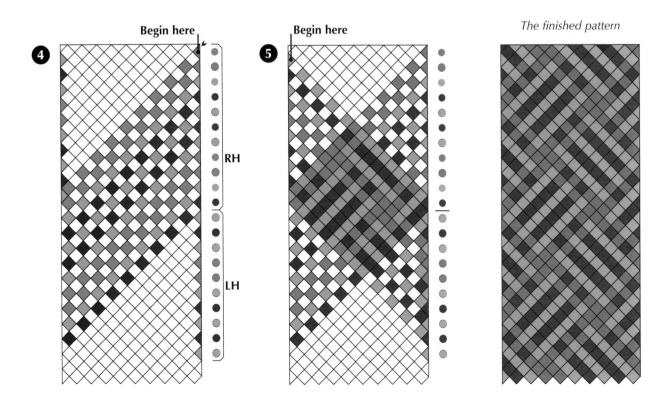

Begin here

4

RH

LH

Begin here

5

The finished pattern

Working with an even number of bobbins Each row of the graph for even-bobbin braids begins and ends with a half-diamond. The width of the braid is determined by counting the spaces across the graph from the right-hand side.

Plain-weave graph widths for even bobbin braids. The graph reads from left to right

20	Bobbins	⋈⋈⋈⋈⋈⋈⋈	10	Spaces
24		⋈⋈⋈⋈⋈⋈⋈⋈	12	
28		⋈⋈⋈⋈⋈⋈⋈⋈⋈	14	
32		⋈⋈⋈⋈⋈⋈⋈⋈⋈⋈	16	
36		⋈⋈⋈⋈⋈⋈⋈⋈⋈⋈⋈	18	
40	⋈⋈⋈⋈⋈⋈⋈⋈⋈⋈⋈⋈⋈		20	

Note: whole and half-diamonds = one space

RULE 2:
When working with an even number of bobbins, the diamond count across the graph equals half the total number of bobbins.

Drawing a Graph

Work through the procedure below to prepare and colour a graph for a three-coloured, 20-bobbin design.

From the Appendix, copy a page of Fig A01. Draw a vertical line down the page to define the right-hand side of the braid. Refer to the graph above and apply Rule 2, counting ten diamond spaces across the graph, and draw the left-hand edge of the braid. The graph should be at least 40 diamonds long in total.

Colouring in the Pattern

Braids with an even number of bobbins are symmetrical. The steps for colouring in these braids are different from the odd-bobbin braids. These braids have a slight ridge down the centre of the braid that is created as the right-hand weft floats over two stitches. (The left-hand weft creates a corresponding float on the underside of the braid.)

When colouring in the pattern, the position of the centre float has to be located on the graph in order to get the pattern to fall correctly across the graph.

1 Transfer the setting-up diagram below to the graph. Note: the right-hand and left-hand edge stitches begin on the same line of the graph opposite each other.

2 Add the left-hand bobbins below the right-hand bobbins, and the right-hand bobbins below the left-hand, in one continuous line, and colour in the edge stitches (figure **(2)** on facing page).

3 Draw a vertical line down the centre of the graph. This helps to locate the floating stitch.

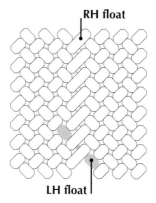
RH float

LH float

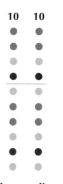
Setting-up diagram

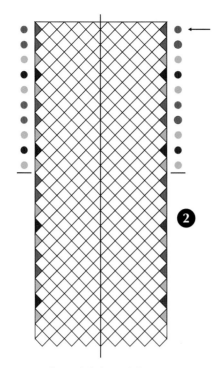

Read graph left to right

4 Work down both sides of the graph, colouring in the first four diamonds until they meet in the centre of the graph, figure **(3)**.

5 Identify the right-hand float at the centre of the graph and colour in these two diamonds.

6 Work down the centre of the braid colouring in all the right-hand floats **(4)**. Continue diagonally and complete colouring in the right-hand stitches until they reach the left-hand edge.

7 Identify where the left-hand float reappears on the graph, colouring in the left-hand stitches until they reach the right-hand edge **(5)**.

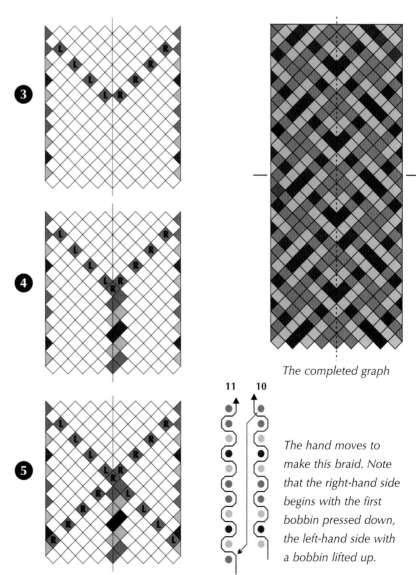

The completed graph

The hand moves to make this braid. Note that the right-hand side begins with the first bobbin pressed down, the left-hand side with a bobbin lifted up.

2/2 Twill Weave Patterns

Twill braids have a distinctive textural appearance: the diagonal pattern is accentuated by vertical ridges known as 'ribbing'. As with plain-weave braids, twill braids can also be made using an odd or even number of bobbins, bringing asymmetry or symmetry to the pattern.

Working with an odd number of bobbins The stitches of 2/2 twill braids are represented on the graph as rectangles. Each stitch moves diagonally passing over two threads from the opposite diagonal.

The narrowest flat twill braid has two vertical ribs and is made with five bobbins. The width of a braid is increased by adding bobbins in units of four, two on each side. This increases the graph width by two columns (ribs). The additional columns are always added to the centre of the graph.

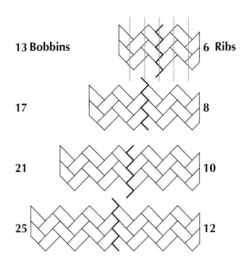

13 Bobbins — 6 Ribs
17 — 8
21 — 10
25 — 12

RULE 3:
The number of vertical ribs is always equal to the left-hand bobbin count.

Drawing a Graph

Copy a page of the master graph in Appendix (Fig A02). Draw a vertical line down the right-hand edge of master graph, count ten spaces across and draw in the left-hand edge.

Colouring in the Pattern

The setting-up diagram below is for a 21-bobbin braid. Colour in the setting-up diagram on the graph as shown, and transfer the left-hand bobbins to the right-hand side.

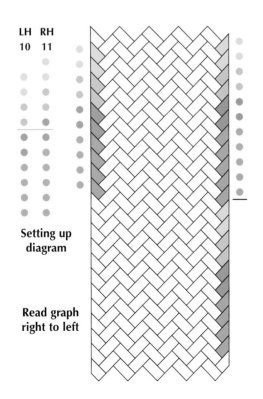

LH   RH
10   11

Setting up diagram

Read graph right to left

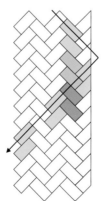

NOTE
When colouring in the graph for twill braids, it is important to be aware how the descending diagonal stitch disappears under two edge stitches before turning in the opposite direction.

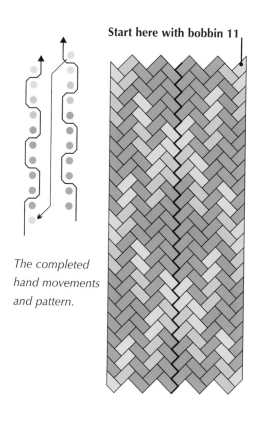

Start here with bobbin 11

The completed hand movements and pattern.

Working with an even number of bobbins The three example graphs **(1)** show a long floating stitch in the centre covering three twill threads. If this is compared with the photograph of the 22-bobbin braid, it will be seen that the floating stitch is hardly discernible. Figure **(2)** shows the braid structure and the position of the floating stitches.

There is no master graph in the Appendix for these braids. A unique graph has to be drawn for each braid width and can be created by adapting Fig A01 (see page 161).

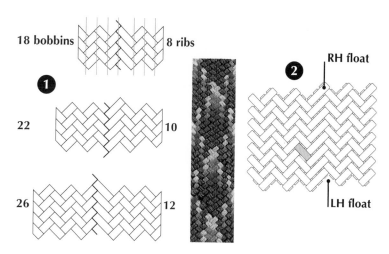

18 bobbins — 8 ribs

1

22 — 10

26 — 12

2

RH float

LH float

Draw a graph for a 22-Bobbin Twill Braid

Draw a vertical line to define the right-hand edge of the braid. Refer to Figure **(1)**, above, for guidance, and construct the graph working toward the left-hand side.

Colouring in the Pattern

1 Transfer the setting-up diagram to the graph. The right-hand and left-hand edge stitches begin on the same line of the graph opposite each other.

2 Add the left-hand bobbins below the right-hand bobbins, and the right-hand bobbins below the left hand, in one continuous line, and colour in the edge stitches.

3 Colour in the setting-up diagram for the 22-bobbin braid onto the graph, transferring the left-hand bobbins to the right-hand side and vice versa. The completed pattern and hand moves are shown on the next page.

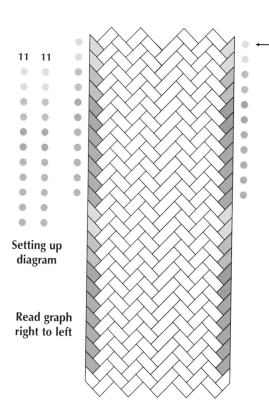

11   11

Setting up diagram

Read graph right to left

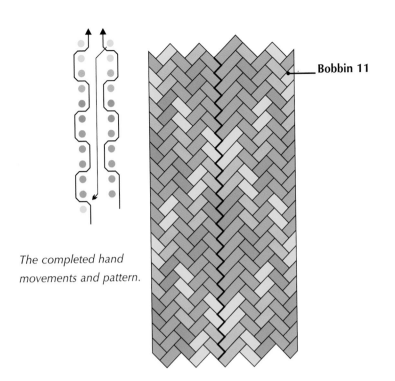

Bobbin 11

The completed hand movements and pattern.

recording your work

Days, weeks or even months after completing a braid there will come a time when you may ask yourself questions about how many ends per bobbin you used, what the position of the point of braiding was, and so on. And, of course, you will have forgotten.

Materials

The application for which a braid is designed usually determines the fibre choice. For example, a braid made from linen will make a strong, firm belt, while rayon gives a good drape for a sash. Braids made from wool may be good for clothing, whereas cotton may be good for curtain trim. Whatever fibre you decide to use for whatever project, it is recommended that fine-count yarns be used in preference to thicker threads. There is no limit to the fibre that can be used; it is up to you to make lots of samples using different yarns, and to record what is made.

Record Sheet

The record sheet is a way to keep information permanently that you will need to know for repeat braids. It brings a greater awareness of the details that need to be kept, whether you are making samples or final projects.

In addition to the record sheet it is helpful to attach a sales tag to your samples with details of the sample and a reference number that brings you back to the record sheet.

Shown below is a list of details that you can choose from to design your own record sheet. Alternatively, you can photocopy the record sheet shown in the appendix (see page 180).

Braid Plan Reference number, date, braid name and description, length, width and end finishes.

Materials Fibre type, size, source and colours. Reason for fibre/colour choice.

Design Detail Snippets of the yarns used can be attached to the record sheet, as can a hand-movement grid or a graphed pattern showing colour ways.

Set-up and Making Method of setting up, position of sword point, weight and number of bobbins, warp length, total weight of yarn and cost, accessories. Time taken warping, setting up, making and finishing, total time taken.

Analysis of Finished Braid
Warp length, warp used, braided length and width, pattern pitch, shrinkage, finishing off detail.

Costing From the above information it is possible to extract details to cost your work. Total yarn used, accessory cost, time taken.

part two:

the designs

plain and colour-and-weave patterns

The setting-up chapter explained that braiding begins on the right-hand side with Step 1 followed by Step 2 on the left. In this and subsequent chapters the designs will call for a greater number of steps to complete a pattern sequence. For example, in design 8 there are eight steps in the sequence.

The five-coloured smaller braids on this jacket by Heather Winslow are made with 25 bobbins, which were arranged in a very different way to that shown in design 1.

Plain Weave Vs Colour and Weave

Plain weave refers to a structure where the threads in the braid warp are alternately lifted one up and one down to create a shed. Colour and weave refers to patterns that are created by arranging light and dark threads in a predetermined repeating sequence. For example, the log-cabin pattern in design 2 is made with a plain weave structure, but the illusion of the striped blocks is created by the repeated sequence of the dark- and light-coloured threads.

In shadow weave, similar striped blocks are changed by altering the structure of the braid. This allows an unlimited ability to alter the pattern within the braid.

Note:
The steps read across the page from right to left, following the natural flow of work.

diamond and five colours

This is the basic plain-weave braid used in the setting-up chapter to explain starting with a tassel. Two designs are shown: a symmetrical diamond shape and a five-coloured diagonal pattern. Simply changing one group of four red bobbins to another colour can change the two-coloured diamond design to a three-coloured design. The five-colour design can be altered in many ways to create your own design.

design 1

25 bobbins

colours:
see set-ups

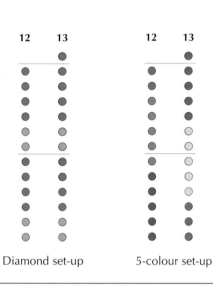

Diamond set-up   5-colour set-up

---

brown and ivory log cabin

The pattern blocks of this log-cabin design change each time a dark thread is repeated. The pattern is made up of a block combination of 3 x 4 x 4. This design was chosen in the setting-up chapter to explain how to create your own designs. The light colour in the block determines the stripes that are seen in the log-cabin patterns; in block 2 two stripes will be seen, and six in block 6. The dark colour accentuates the stripes. Each block begins with two dark bobbins followed by alternating light and dark bobbins.

design 2

25 bobbins

colours:
● 14
○ 11

2-colour set-up

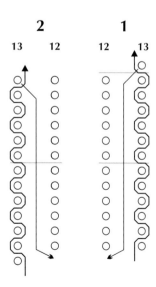

design 3   2- and 3-colour offset log-cabin variation

30 bobbins

colours: see set-ups

This braid is made with an even number of bobbins. It produces an offset pattern variation of the log cabin. The hand moves on the right-hand side begin with lifting a bobbin up on the back of the hand, whereas on the left-hand side the first bobbin is pressed down.

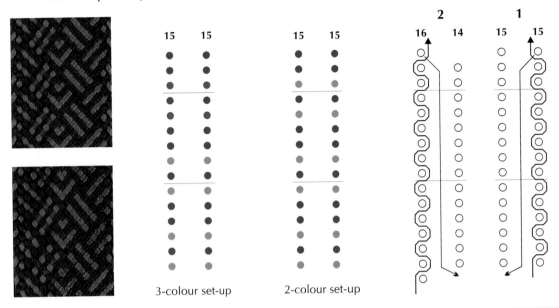

3-colour set-up   2-colour set-up

design 4   log cabin with hand-move variation

30 bobbins

colours: see set-ups

In design 4, the hand moves for both sides of the braid begin with the first bobbin pressed down.

2-colour set-up   3-colour set-up

hound's tooth

Design 5 and 6 both are well-known weaving patterns.

2   **1**

| 20 | 20 | 21 | 19 | 20 | 20 |

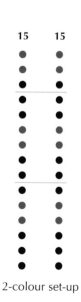

2-colour set-up

design 5

40 bobbins

colours:
- ● 20
- ● 20

---

hound's tooth variation

2   **1**

| 15 | 15 | 16 | 14 | 15 | 15 |

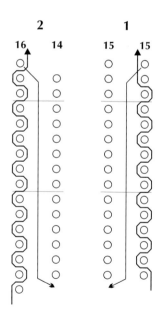

2-colour set-up

design 6

30 bobbins

colours:
- ● 18
- ● 12

design 7 3-colour log cabin

48 bobbins

Design 7 further develops the log cabin into a three-coloured braid.

colours:
see set-up 48

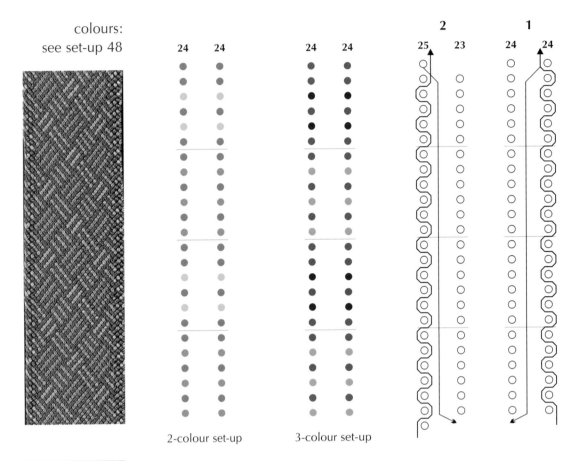

2-colour set-up   3-colour set-up

diamond design with changing centre patterns   design 8

This pattern shows how to change the structure of the braid as it is worked, altering the pattern in the centre of the diamond.

32 bobbins

4 colours:
- 10
- 10
- 8
- 4

Change to Pattern 3 when blue No.10 bobbins in Pattern 2 reach the No.16 position. Then go directly to hand moves 5 and 6.

Pattern 2

4   **3**

17   15   16   **16**   16   16

		10	
		9	
		8	
		7	
		6	
		5	
		4	
		3	
		2	
		1	
		16	
		15	
		14	
		13	
		12	
		11	

Set-up

Make the change to Pattern 2 when the blue No.10 bobbins reach the No.16 position. Then go directly to the hand moves 3 and 4.

Pattern 1

2   **1**

17   15   16   **16**   16   16

		16	
		15	
		14	
		13	
		12	
		11	
		10	
		9	
		8	
		7	
		6	
		5	
		4	
		3	
		2	
		1	

Set-up

Revert to Pattern 1 when blue No.10 bobbins in Pattern 4 reach the No.16 position. Then go directly to hand moves 1 and 2.

Pattern 3

8   **7**

17   15   16   **16**

Change to Pattern 4 when blue No.10 bobbins in Pattern 3 reach the No.16 position. Then go directly to hand moves 7 and 8.

Pattern 4

6   **5**

17   15   16   **16**

design 9   shadow weave

44 bobbins

2 colours:
22 ○
22 ●

Design 9 is derived from a loom-weaving structure called 'shadow weave'. Unlike the log cabin, where blocks change when two threads of the same colour are repeated in a pattern block, shadow-weave blocks are changed by altering the structure of the braid. This gives great flexibility in designing patterns.

The heavy line shown at the side of the hand moves shows when a twill move is made in the plain-weave sequence, changing the pattern blocks. The twill move in this design is separated by 9 and 10 plain-weave bobbins. If, for example, the twill move were altered to separate 8 or 12 bobbins, it would result in quite a different pattern.

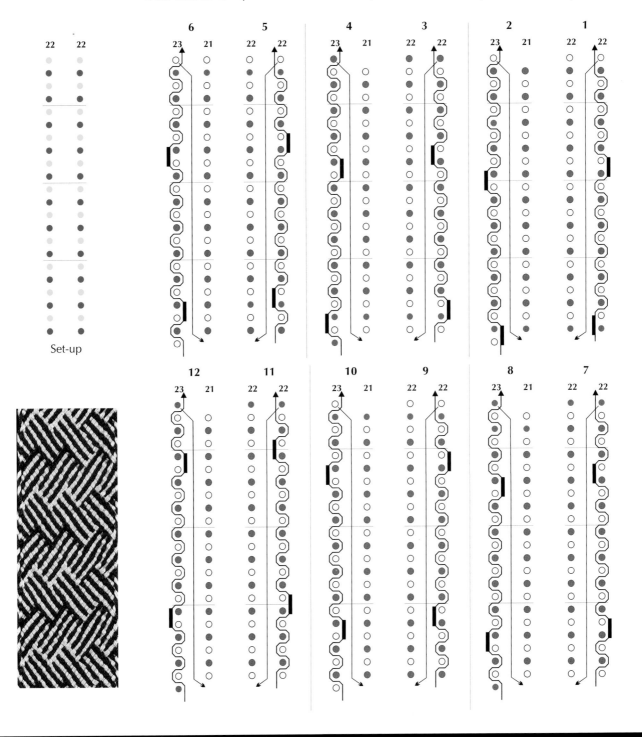

Set-up

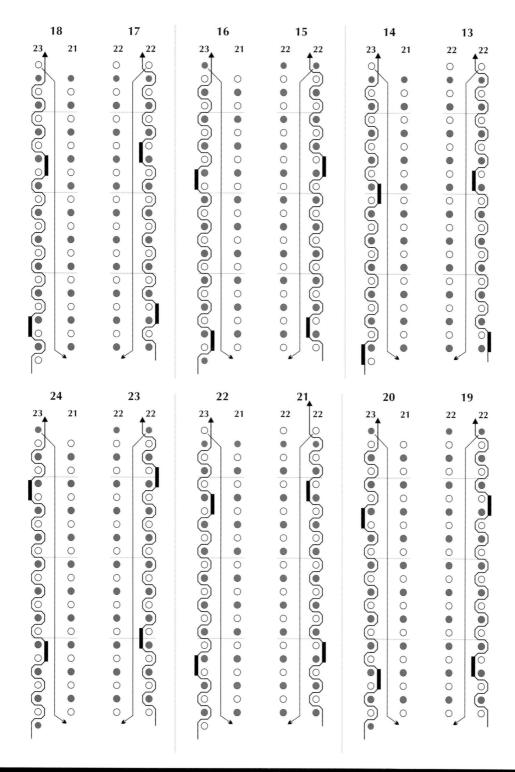

design 10 plain and twill weave

33 bobbins

1 colour:

33 ●

Design 10 combines plain and twill weave. It was used in the setting-up chapter to explain starting a braid with a loop. In addition to making an overall pattern and one down the centre of the braid, the design can also be made down one side leaving the other side plain twill weave.

Overall pattern

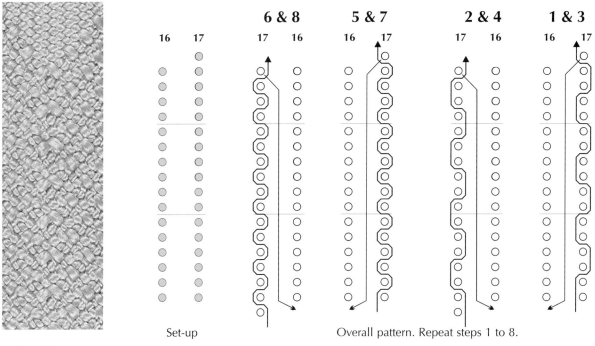

Set-up

6 & 8 **5 & 7** **2 & 4** **1 & 3**

Overall pattern. Repeat steps 1 to 8.

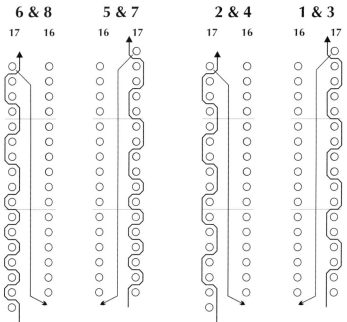

Centre pattern

6 & 8 **5 & 7** **2 & 4** **1 & 3**

Centre pattern. Repeat steps 1 to 8.

2/2 twill weave

This is a 25-bobbin 2/2 twill braid. It uses the same arrangement of five colours as was used in design 1 and also in design 13, a 25-bobbin 3/3 twill braid. If the three braids are compared it will be seen how the pattern changes as the width of the braid narrows.

design 11

25 bobbins

5 colours:
see set-up

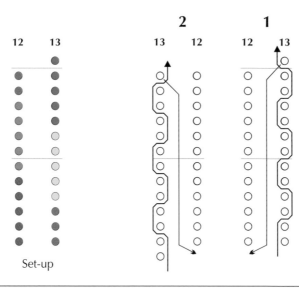

Set-up

3-colour 2/2 twill weave

Design 12 shows a three-colour variation of a 2/2 twill braid made with 37 bobbins. Extending the number of bobbins always increases the pattern possibilities.

design 12

37 bobbins

5 and 7 colours:
see set-up

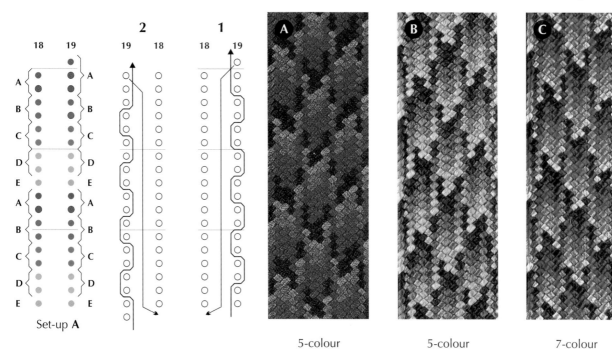

Set-up A

A 5-colour

B 5-colour

C 7-colour

design 13   3/3 twill weave

25 bobbins

colours:
see set-ups

Chevron

5-colour

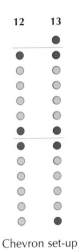

12   13

Chevron set-up

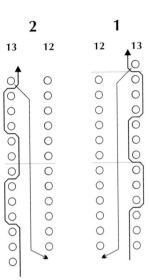

2   **1**

13   12   12   13

12   13

5-colour set-up

rep braids

Try using a warp made up of multiple fine yarns using mercerized cotton, rayon or silk to bring out the lustre in these braids and emphasize their ridged texture.

A rep braid is a warp-faced interlaced braid. The structure of these braids creates ridges that reflect light and accentuate shadow, and this is an important part of their design. The ridges in these braids are formed by the concealment of multiple warps, which are covered and hidden by the wefts or by closely woven wefts over single warps. It is a combination of these elements, repeated in various sequences, that creates the patterns.

There are a lot of opportunities to experiment when making rep braids. For example, many pre-Hispanic Peruvian braids can be adapted and made on the takadai, as the Peruvian turban braid made by Terry Flynn illustrates.

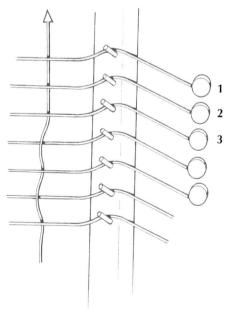

The hand passes under three warp threads at the end of the shed in design 14. These three warps then become wefts and are cast through the shed in the order shown (1–3). At Step 1 in designs 18 and 19 the wefts are cast in the reverse order (3–1).

design 14   chevron

36 bobbins

5 colours:
6 ○
6 ○
6 ○
6 ●
12 ○

The ribs seen in designs 14 to 17 are plain weave with multiple wefts made with one or more colours.

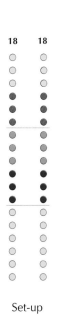

Set-up

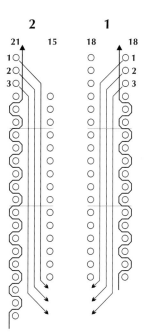

---

design 15   1- and 6-colour rep braids

43 bobbins

colours:
see set-ups

It is interesting to compare these two braids. At first glance they appear to be two different braids. This is because the one-colour braid shows a 'V' ridge pattern, but when additional colours are added to the design this reverses to show an 'A' pattern.

1-colour set-up

6-colour set-up

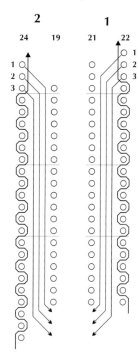

chevron blocks and outlines

4   **3**   **2**   **1**

21   24

3-colour set-up

8   **7**   **6**   **5**

21   24

5-colour set-up

design 16

45 bobbins

colours:
see set-ups

design 16

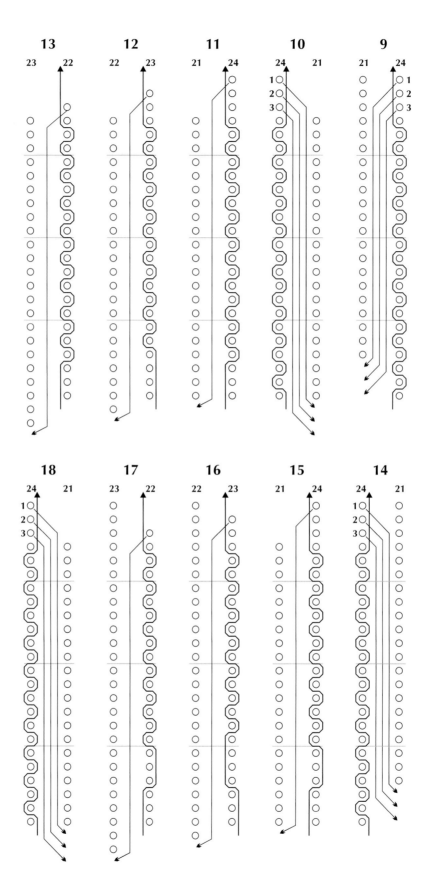

rep braid with linked edges   design 17

42 bobbins

3 colours:
- 36
- 3
- 3

	5		**2 & 4**		**1 & 3**	
21	21	21	21	18	21	21

Set-up

KOMA CHANGE POSITION:
After Step 4 bring both empty koma to the front of the arms.

Step 5 exchange koma A with koma B.

Working one side at a time lift koma A off the arm, push koma B forward, return koma A to the arm behind koma B.

design 18   lattice design

36 bobbins

colours:
see set-ups

2-colour

3-colour

Designs 18 to 24 are made with a combination of twill and plain-weave hand movements. Here is a tip to speed up the braiding of design 18:

Design 18 is made with a combination of 3/3 twill and plain-weave hand moves. Make Step 1 casting the weft. Beat the shed but leave the sword in the shed, which makes it easier to see the hand moves for Step 2. Now pick up the opposite set of threads, insert the sword into the new shed, cast the weft and beat. The same applies for Step 3. Note also how the weft threads for steps 1 to 6 are cast in a different sequence to those for steps 7 to 10.

2-colour set-up

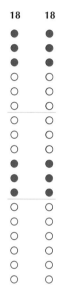

3-colour set-up

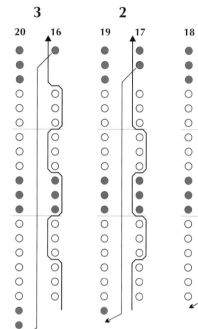

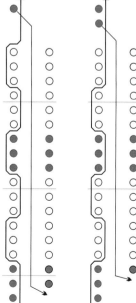

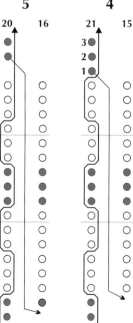

self-coloured diamonds

36 bobbins

1 colour:
⬤ 36

18   **18**

4,10,16   **3,9,15**   **2,8,14**   **1,7,13**

21   15   20   16   19   17   18   18

Set-up

20,22,24   **19,21,23**   **6,12,18**   **5,11,17**

21   15   18   18   19   17   20   16

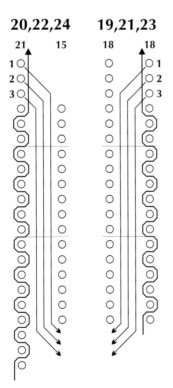
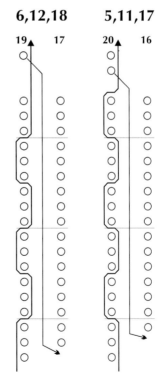

design 20   chevron with centre ridge

43 bobbins

1 colour:
43 ●

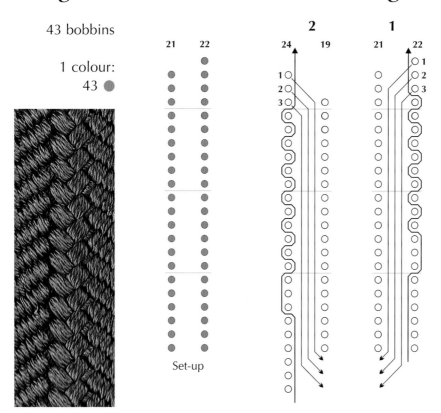

Set-up

design 21   broken chevron

45 bobbins

1 colour:
45 ●

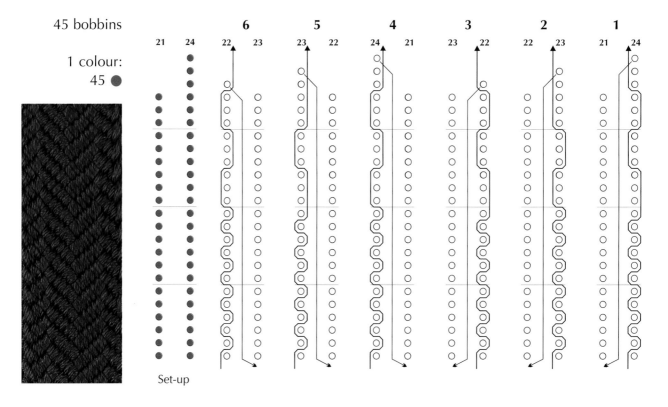

Set-up

waves

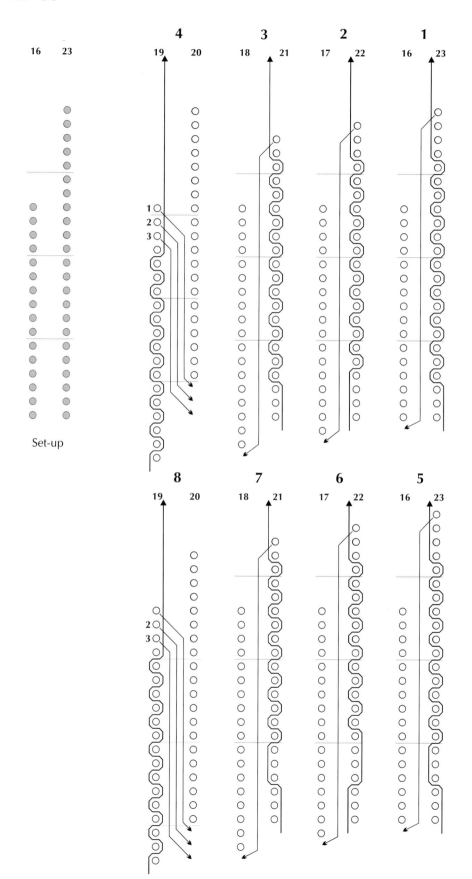

Set-up

design 22

39 bobbins

1 colour:
● 39

design 22

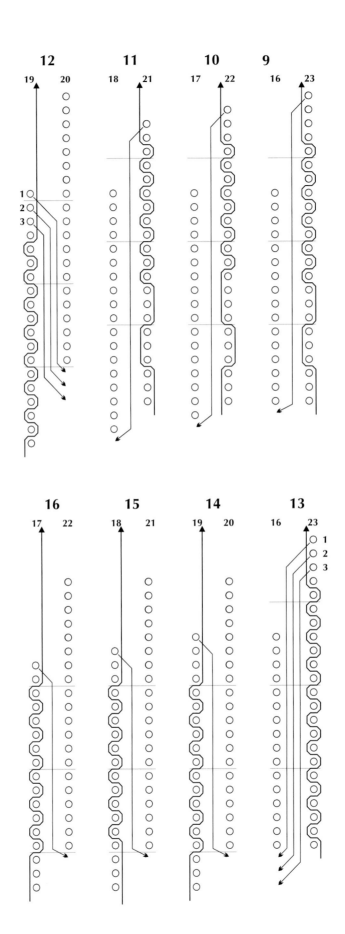

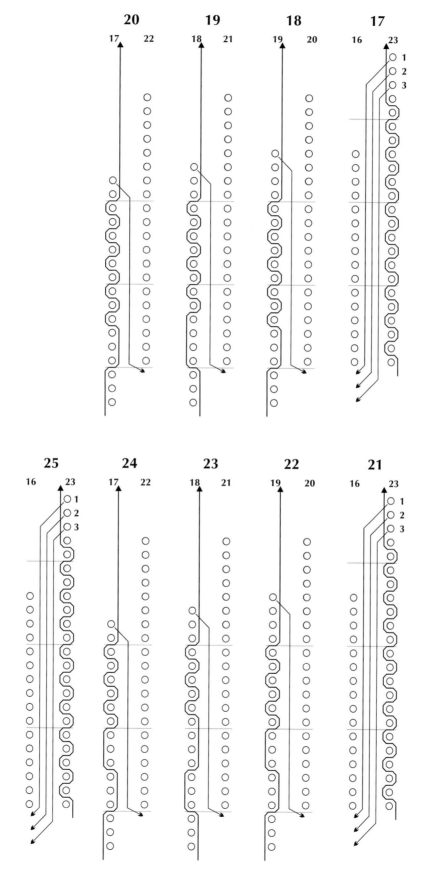

design 23

36 bobbins

1 colour:

36 ⬤

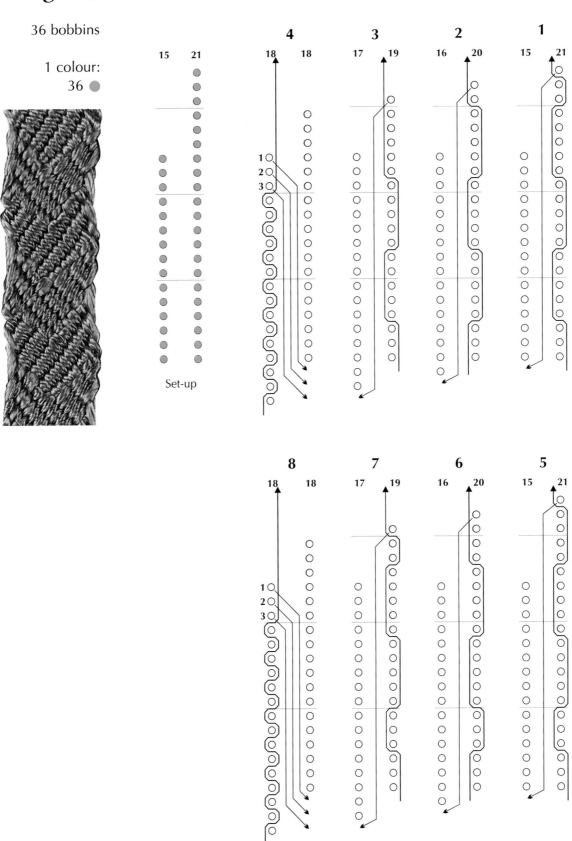

Set-up

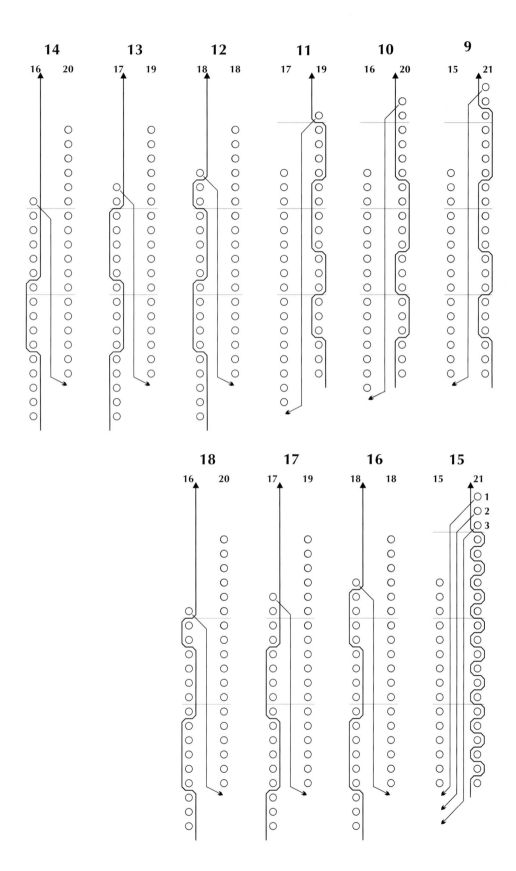

design 23

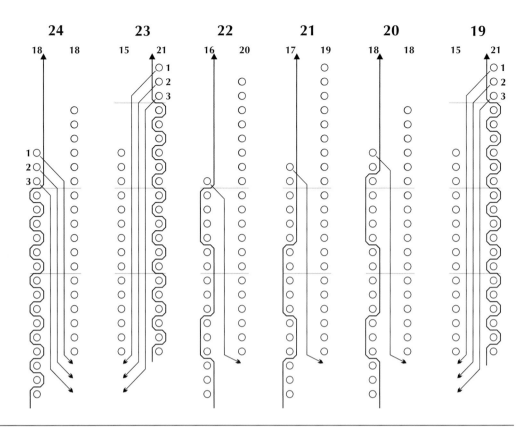

design 24

37 bobbins

1 colour:
37 ⬤

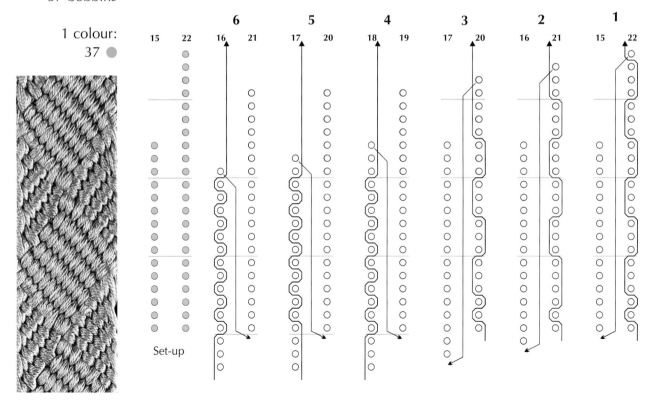

Set-up

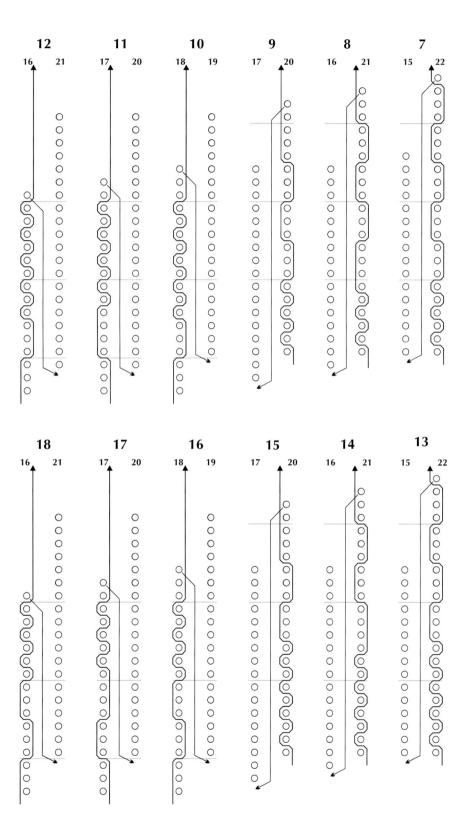

design 24

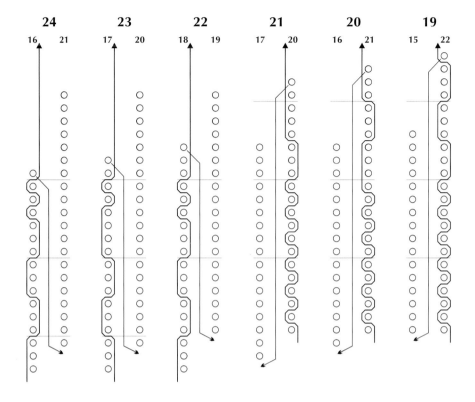

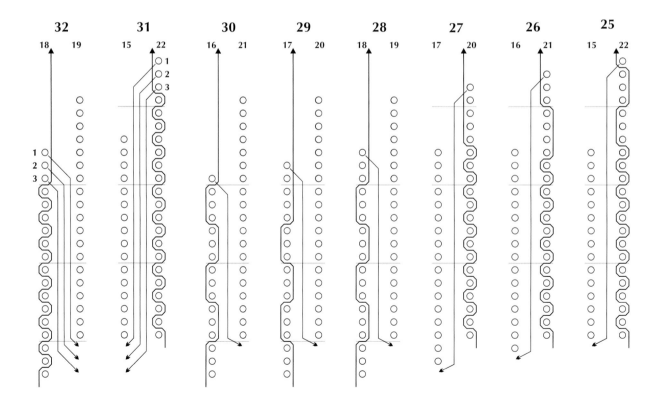

Designs 25 to 27 have selected warps that are of a different colour to the majority of the warp, and this creates a pattern within the rep braid. It is possible to create new designs by changing the position of the selected warp threads, or by changing colours as will be seen in the three pattern variations in design 27.

48 bobbins

2 colours:
● 36
● 12

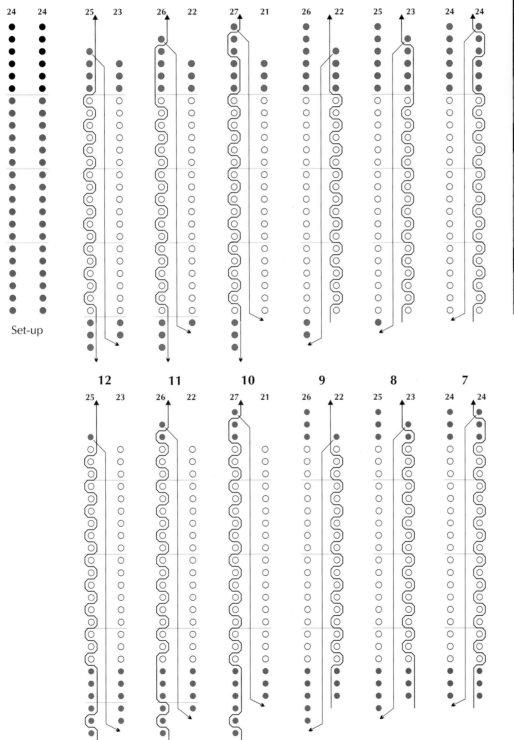

design 25

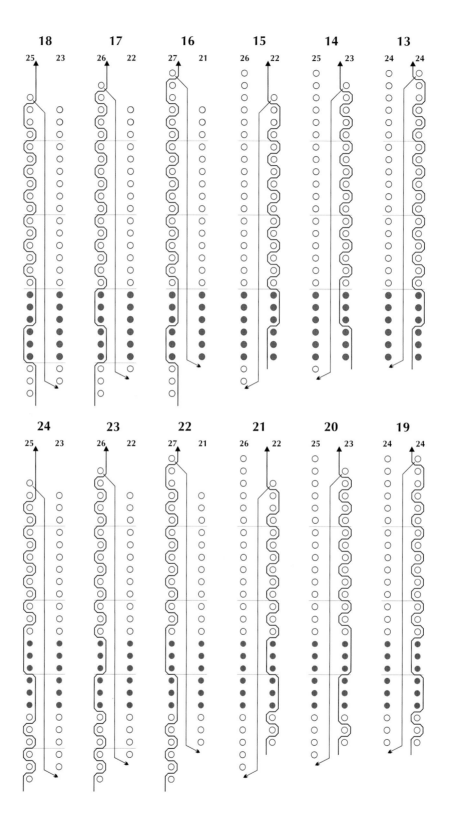

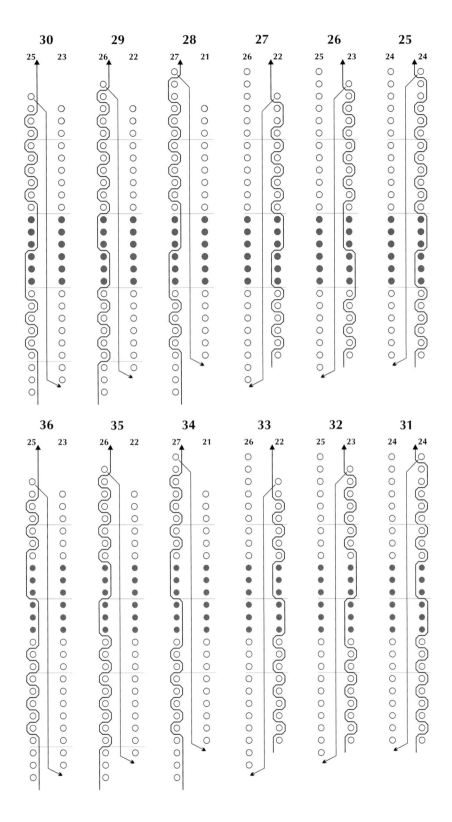

design 25

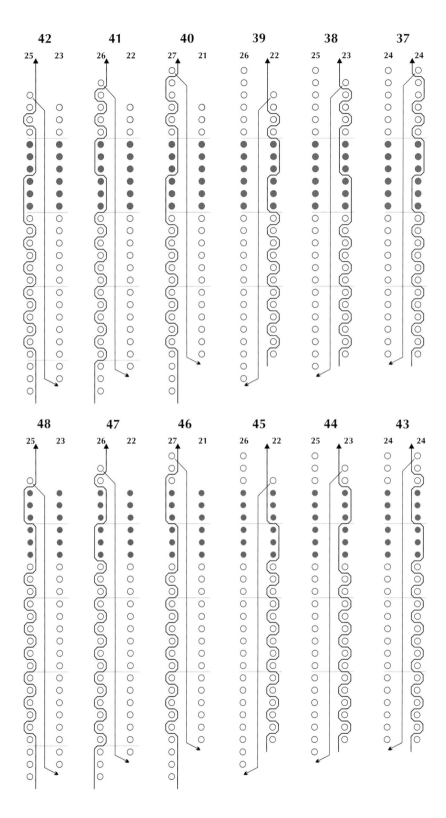

design 26

48 bobbins

2 colours:
- ● 40
- ● 8

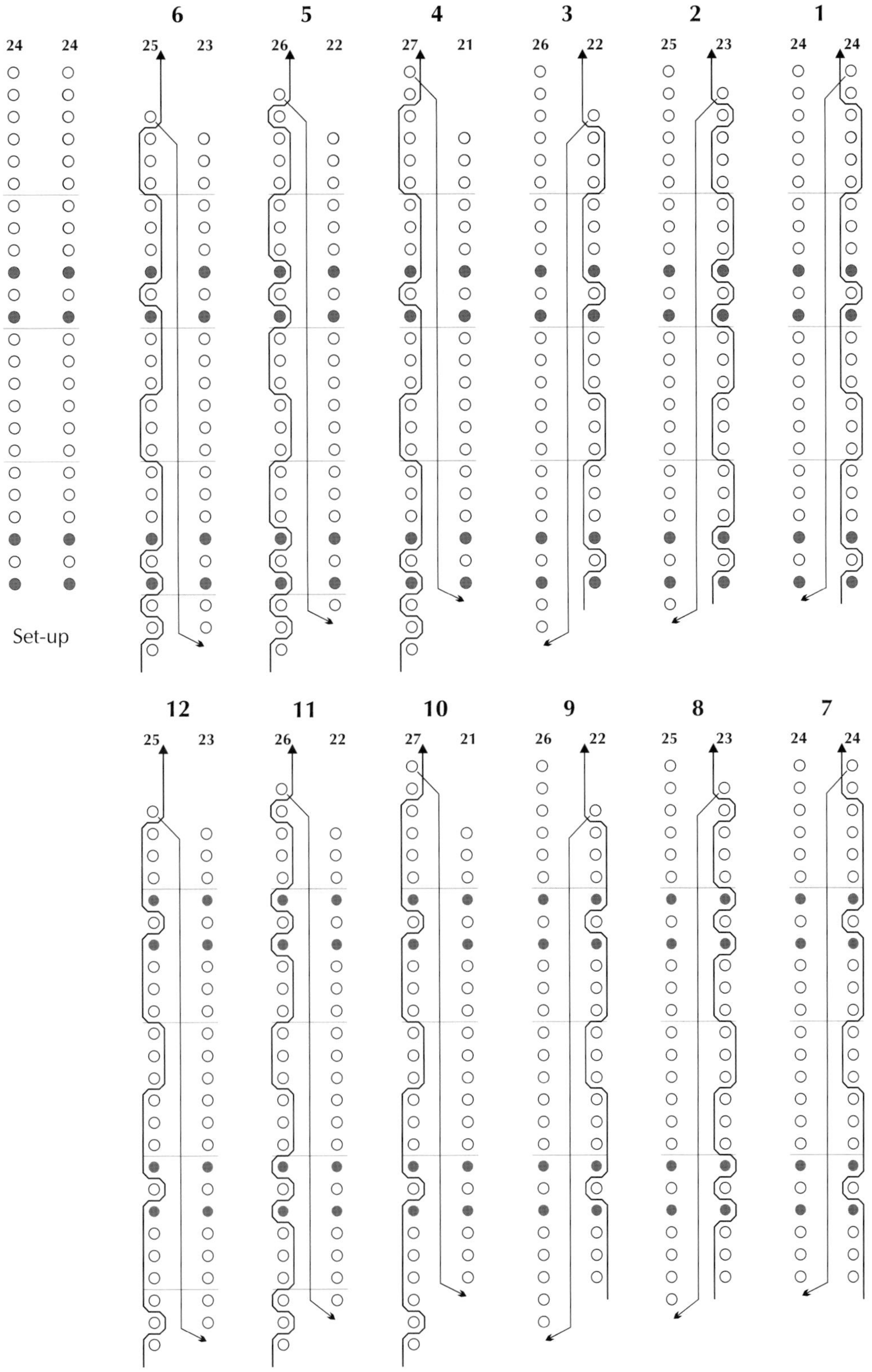

Set-up

design 26

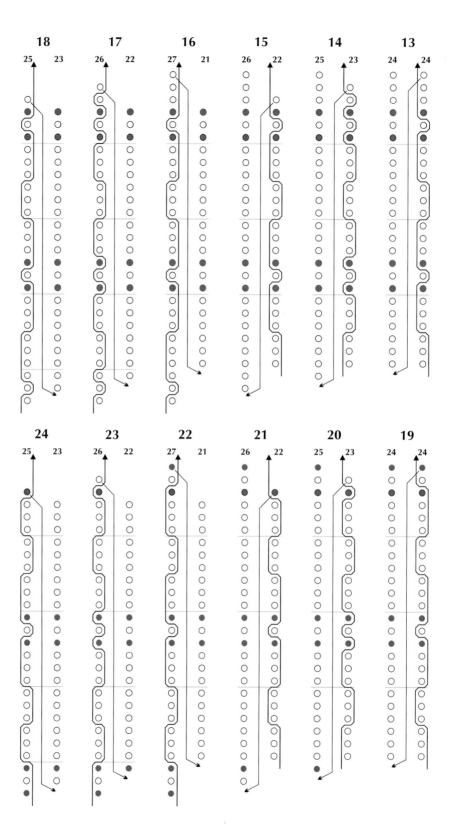

making kumihimo japanese interlaced braids

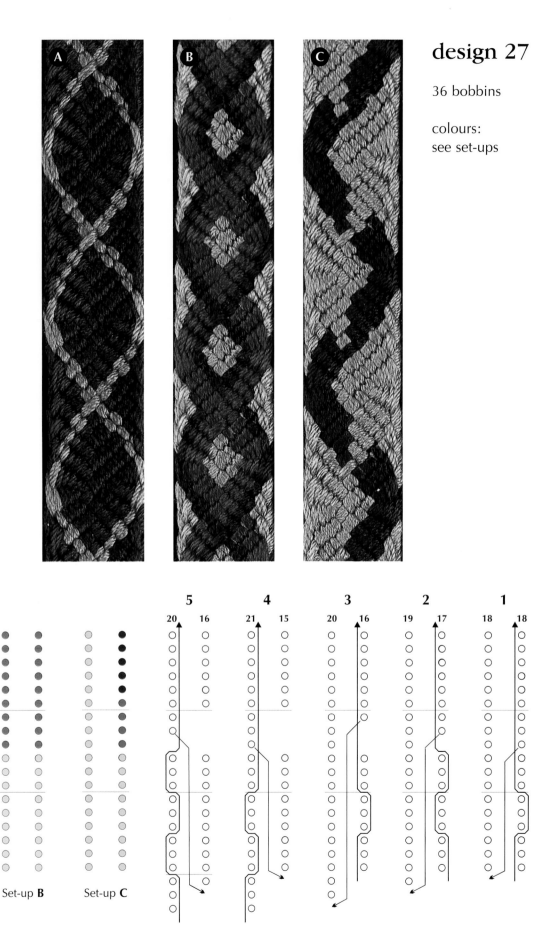

design 27

36 bobbins

colours:
see set-ups

Set-up **A**   Set-up **B**   Set-up **C**

design 27

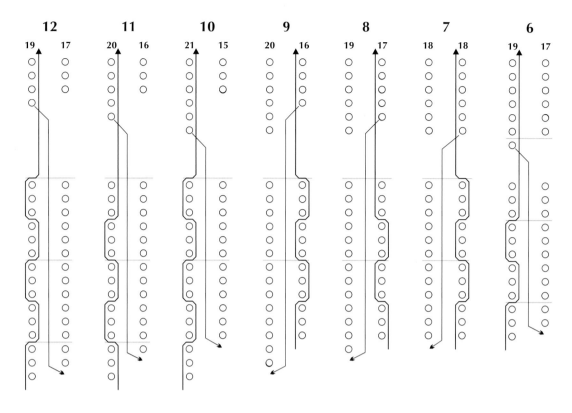

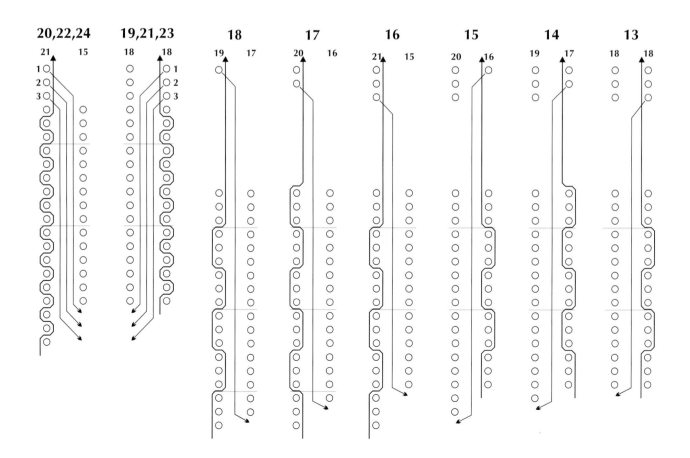

making kumihimo japanese interlaced braids

design 28

Design 28 is a two-coloured braid. As there are 70 hand moves to complete one pattern cycle it is useful to apply the tip given in design 18. Two designs are shown: braid 'A' is the original and varying the sequence of hand moves created braid 'B'. This is similar to how changes can be made in a shadow-weave braid.

48 bobbins

colours:
○ 24
● 24

Left Hand			Right Hand				Left Hand			Right Hand		
12	11	10	9	8	7		6	5	4	3	2	1
23	24	25	24	25	26		23	24	25	24	25	26

Set-up

To make design A takes two repeats of the 70 steps to return to the setting-up pattern.

To make design B the continuous diamond pattern repeat steps 1 to 18, then 43 to 60.

Left Hand			Right Hand				Left Hand			Right Hand		
24	23	22	21	20	19		18	17	16	15	14	13
23	24	25	24	25	26		23	24	25	24	25	26

design 28

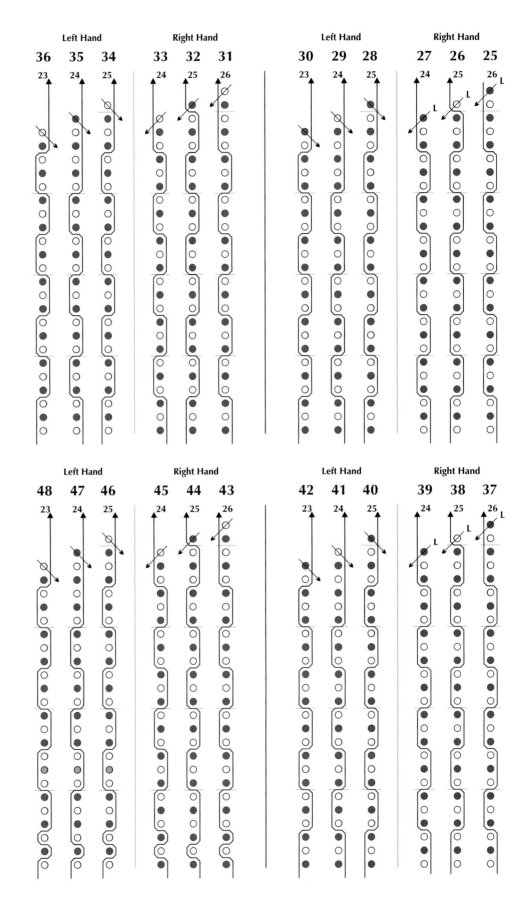

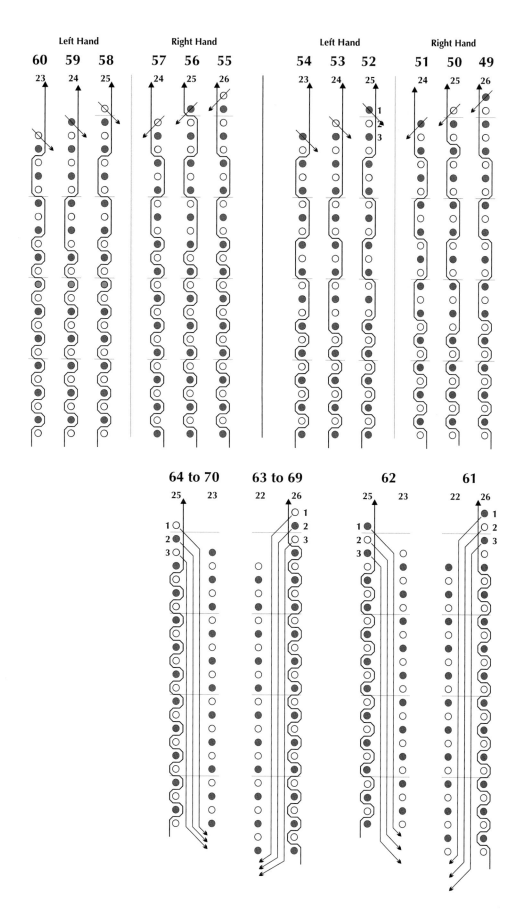

design 29   plain weave

39 bobbins

1 colour:

39 ○

Design 29 is in between a single and a double braid as it uses both upper and lower arms during the process of braiding. This braid can be made in at least two colours and the texture of the structure can be varied. Try setting up the braid in two colours, one for right-hand side and one for the left-hand side.

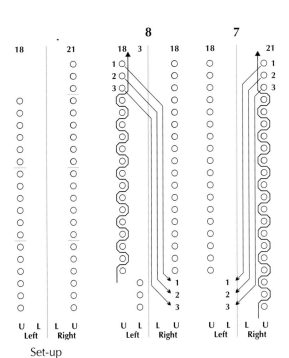

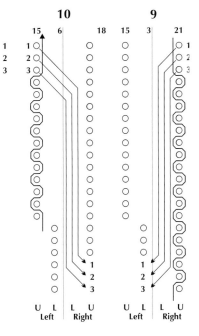

Step 18. After completing the move, transfer all the bobbins on the left-hand lower arm to the upper arm.

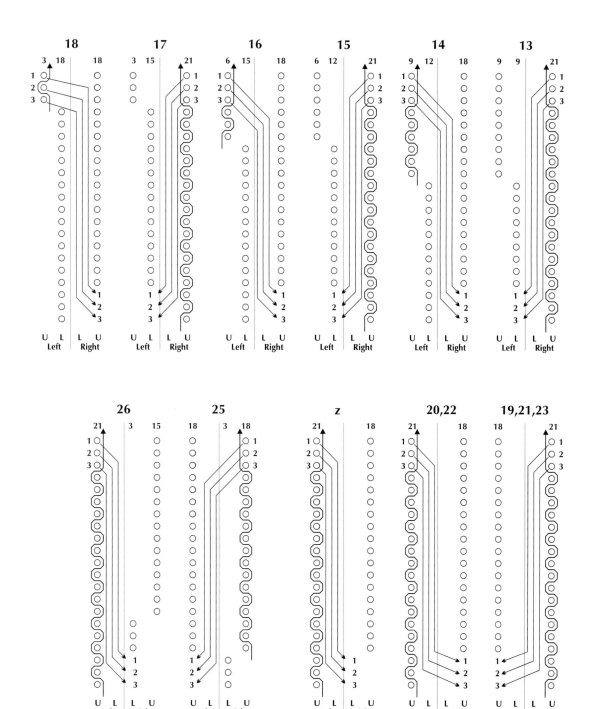

design 29

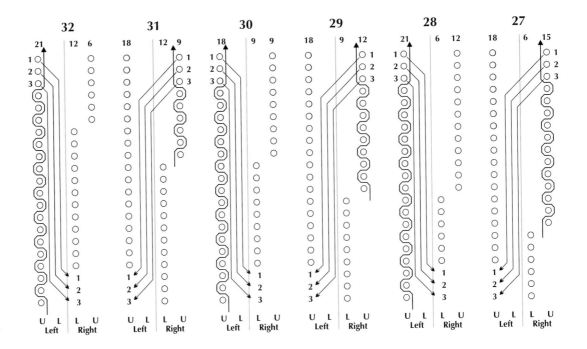

Step 36. After completing the move, transfer all the bobbins from the right-hand lower arm to the upper arm.

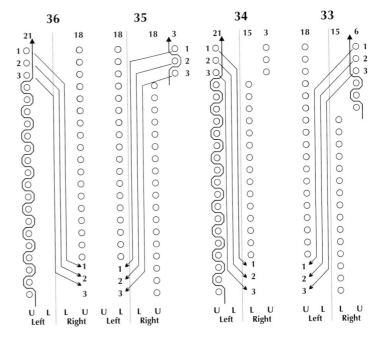

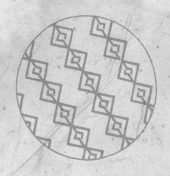

adding edge and centre pattern

This section of the book shows how to add a plain or patterned stripe to the design, either at the edges or along the centre of the braid.

When made with fine threads, this embellishment method creates braids that are very elegant and ribbon-like in appearance, making excellent bookmarks or trimming for clothing. Adding an edge colour to a belt outlines the design, and beads threaded on to the tassels of a sash give an extra swinging drape.

This belt was made with the edge twining method used in design 33 (see page 105).

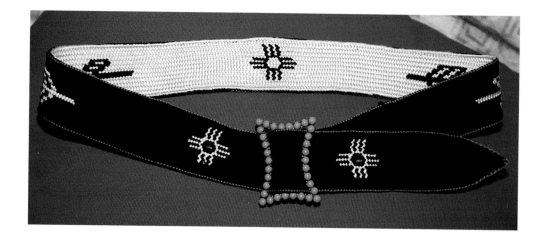

design 30   feathered centre ridge: plain weave

29 bobbins

1 colour:
29 ⬤

Designs 30 to 32 show how to add a pattern to the centre of the braid, techniques that can be used with any plain weave or twill structure.

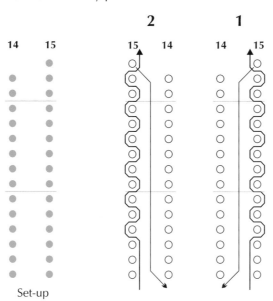

Set-up

The central ridge in this design is created by lifting up the first three bobbins on the back of the hand.

The width of the ridge can be increased by lifting four or five bobbins at the beginning of the shed.

---

design 31   centre twining: alternating twill weave

31 bobbins

2 colours:
29 ◯
2 ⬤

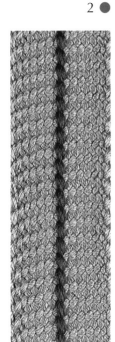

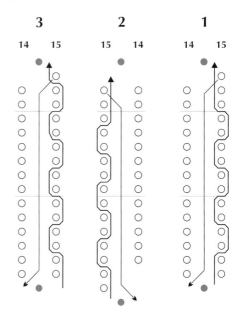

Set-up

The pattern that runs down the centre of this braid is made by twining the dark-coloured No.1 bobbins. When all the bobbins are arranged on the takadai, place one twining bobbin over the torii, and let the other hang down below the warp so that it lies against the sword stick. These bobbins are worked separately from the main warp.

Note how the hand moves to make a shed at steps 1 and 2 differ from those in steps 3 and 4.

Step 5. Hold the thread on the torii with the right hand and hold the other bobbin thread in the left. Turn your hands in a clockwise direction, twining the two bobbins together so they change place.

centre twining: twill weave

design 32

33 bobbins

14   15

When all the bobbins are arranged on the takadai, place two No.1 dark bobbins over the torii and let the No.2 bobbins hang down below the warp so that they lay against the sword stick. The dark bobbins are worked separately from the main warp.

Work steps 1 and 2, and then Step 3.

Twine the dark bobbins. Bring the bobbins on the torii down and place them between the lower pair. Lift the lower pair up and place them on the torii.

Set-up

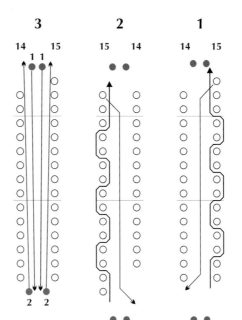

2 colours:
- ⚪ 29
- ⚪ 4

---

twill weave with coloured edge

design 33

Design 33 is a one-coloured twill braid with coloured edges. The edge colour is made by twining pairs of bobbins together as the braid is worked.

33 bobbins

2 colours:
- ⚪ 29
- ⚫ 4

16   17

The dark bobbins at the top of the warp twine over the weft after it has been cast through the shed, creating a coloured edge stitch that appears on the underside of the braid.

At Step 3 the twining bobbins are repositioned ready for the next Step 1 and 2 moves.

Set-up

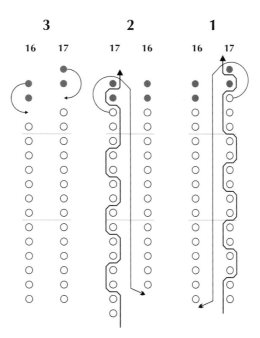

design 34　log cabin with border

25 bobbins

2 colours:
15 ⬤
10 ⬤

The threads for the edges of designs 34 to 37 are worked as separate braids and linked to the main braid as the weft is cast through the shed. There are two methods for linking, one for braids with an odd number of bobbins (designs 34 and 35) and one for working with an even number of bobbins (designs 36 and 37). The number of edge threads in these designs has been limited to six on either side, but extra threads can be added (always in an even number) to increase the width.

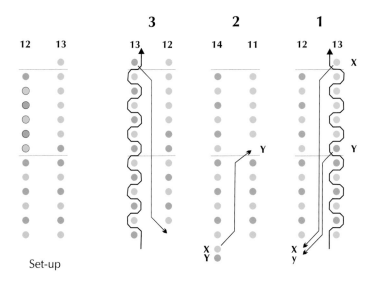

Set-up

Right Hand:
Step 1. Make a plain weave shed. Cast bobbin marked X through the shed to the opposite koma in front of bobbin number 1 (see Fig A). Cast bobbin marked Y through the shed to lower left-hand koma in front of X (see Fig A).

Step 2. Return bobbin X through the shed to the space vacated by the Y bobbin and beat. This will link the X and Y threads together as shown in Fig B.

Left Hand:
Step 3 shows the left-hand move.

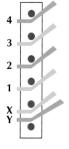

Fig A　　　　　　Fig B

log cabin with border

design 35

33 bobbins

3 colours:
- 12
- 12
- 9

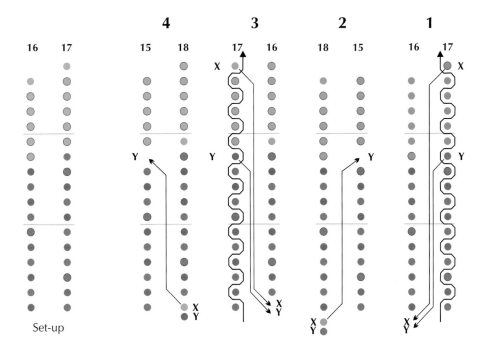

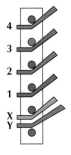

Set-up

Right- and Left-hand Steps:

Step 1. Make a plain-weave shed. Cast bobbin marked X through the shed to opposite lower koma in front of bobbin No.1 (see Fig A). Cast the pattern bobbin marked Y through the shed to lower left-hand koma in front of X (see Fig A).

Step 2. Return bobbin X through the shed to the space vacated by the Y bobbin and beat. This will link the X and Y threads together as shown in Fig B.

Steps 3 and 4 show the left-hand moves.

Fig A

Fig B

design 36 hound's tooth with border

36 bobbins

3 colours:
12 ●
12 ●
12 ●

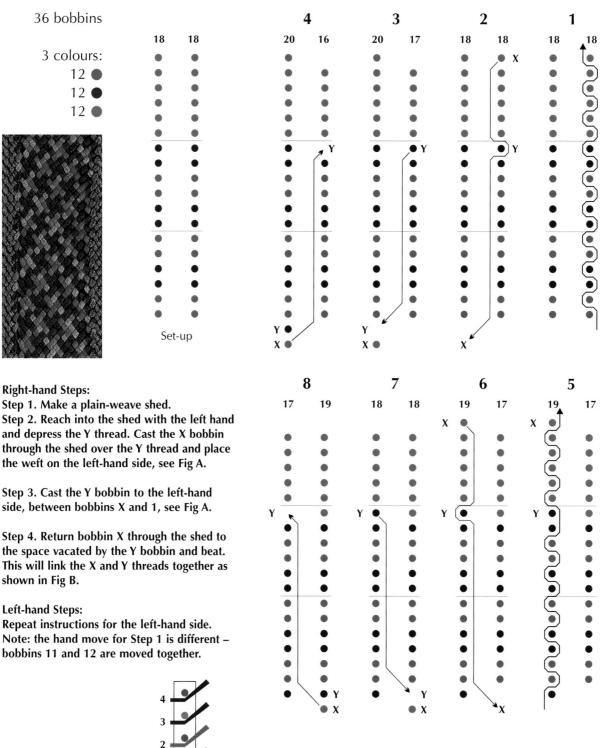

Set-up

Right-hand Steps:
Step 1. Make a plain-weave shed.
Step 2. Reach into the shed with the left hand and depress the Y thread. Cast the X bobbin through the shed over the Y thread and place the weft on the left-hand side, see Fig A.

Step 3. Cast the Y bobbin to the left-hand side, between bobbins X and 1, see Fig A.

Step 4. Return bobbin X through the shed to the space vacated by the Y bobbin and beat. This will link the X and Y threads together as shown in Fig B.

Left-hand Steps:
Repeat instructions for the left-hand side.
Note: the hand move for Step 1 is different – bobbins 11 and 12 are moved together.

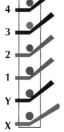

Fig A   Fig B

hound's tooth with border   design 37

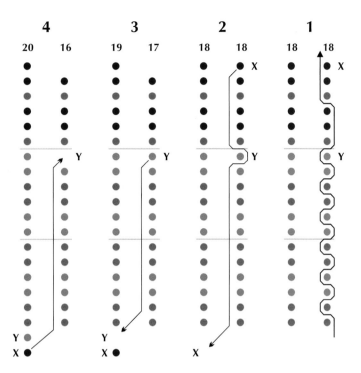

33 bobbins

4 colours:
- ● 12
- ● 12
- ● 8
- ● 4

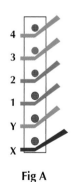

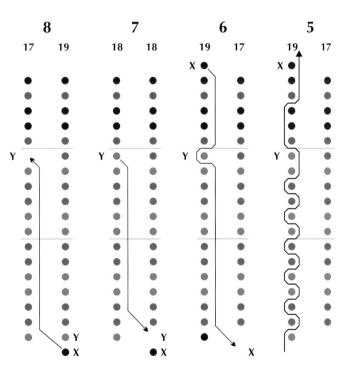

Right-hand Steps:
Step 1. Make a plain-weave shed.
Step 2. Reach into the shed with the left hand and depress the Y thread. Cast the X bobbin through the shed over the Y thread and place the weft on the left-hand side (see Fig A).

Step 3. Cast the Y bobbin to the left-hand side, between bobbins X and 1 (see Fig A).

Step 4. Return bobbin X through the shed to the space vacated by the Y bobbin and beat. This will link the X and Y threads together as shown in Fig B.

Left-hand Steps:
Repeat these instructions for the left-hand side, but note that the hand move for Step 1 is different. Bobbins 11 and 12 are moved together.

Fig A

Fig B

design 38 itsukushima

38 bobbins

4 colours:

14 ●
12 ○
6 ◐
6 ●

Itsukushima is the name given to this Japanese temple braid. The original dating from the twelfth century would have been made by loop manipulation. The braid was discovered in a shrine near Hiroshima wrapped around a Buddhist sutra scroll. This version braided on the takadai is a modern interpretation taking 40 steps to complete one pattern sequence and 80 steps to return to the setting-up position. The 40 steps are divided into four groups of moves: Step 1 repeated ten times, Step 2 repeated nine times, Step 3 repeated ten times, and Step 4 repeated 11 times.

			1–3		1–2		1–1		1	
19	19		21	17	20	18	19	19	19	19

Set-up

Step .1 Repeat this sequence ten times.

Step 1. Make a right-hand shed as shown.

Step 1–1. With the left hand, reach into the shed and push down the warp thread marked Y. Cast the bobbin marked X through the shed over the Y thread and place the weft two spaces down from the first left-hand warp (see Fig A).

Step 1–2. Cast the Y bobbin to the left-hand side, between bobbins X and 1 (see Fig A).

Step 1–3. Return bobbin X through the shed to the space vacated by the Y bobbin and beat. This will link the X and Y together as shown in Fig B.

Steps 1–4 to 1–7 show the left-hand bobbin moves.

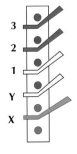

Fig A
Left-hand koma

Fig B
Right-hand linking

Position of bobbins after completing ten steps.

1–7   **1–6**   **1–5**   **1–4**

Position of bobbins after completing 19 steps.

2–2   **2–1**   Step 2. Repeat this sequence nine times.

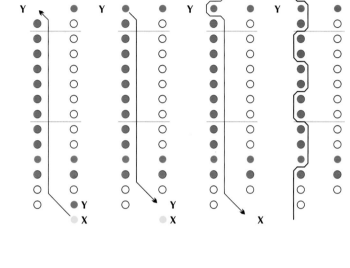

design 38

Step 3. Repeat this sequence ten times.

Step 3. Make a right-hand shed as shown.

Step 3–1. With the left hand push down the warp thread marked Z. Cast the bobbin marked X through the shed over the Z thread and place the weft two spaces down from the first left-hand warp (see Fig C).

Step 3–2. Lift the bobbin marked Z over to the left-hand side and place the bobbin between bobbin X and 1 (see Fig C).

Step 3–3. Lift bobbin X over to the right-hand side into the space vacated by the Z bobbin and beat. This will link the X and Z together as shown in Fig D.

Steps 3–4 to 3–7 show the left-hand bobbin moves.

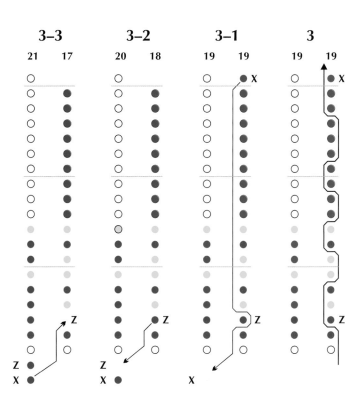

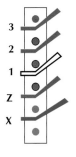

Fig C
Left-hand koma

Fig. D
Right-hand linking

Position of bobbins after completing 29 steps.

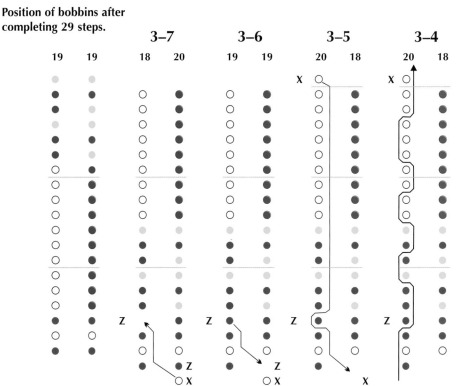

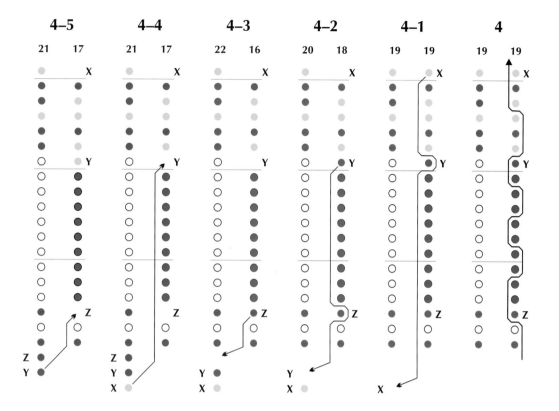

Step 4. Repeat this sequence 11 times.

Step 4. Make a right-hand shed as shown.

Step 4–1. With the left hand reach into the shed and push down the warp thread marked Y. Cast the bobbin marked X through the shed over the Y thread and place the weft on the left-hand koma three spaces down from the first left-hand bobbin (see Fig E).

Step 4–2. Push down the Z thread and cast the bobbin marked Y through the shed over the Z thread and place the weft on the left-hand koma two spaces down from the first left-hand bobbin.

Step 4–3. Lift the Z thread over to the left-hand side and place in front of the left-hand No. 1 bobbin.

Step 4–4. Cast the bobbin marked X from the left-hand koma back through the shed and place in the space vacated by the Y thread. This will link the X and Y threads together (see Fig E).

Step 4–5. Lift the bobbin on the left-hand koma marked Y over to the right-hand side into the place vacated by the Z bobbin and beat. Fig F shows how the X, Y and Z threads are linked together.

Fig E

Left-hand koma

Fig F

Right-hand linking

design 38

**Bobbin position
after completing
40 steps.**

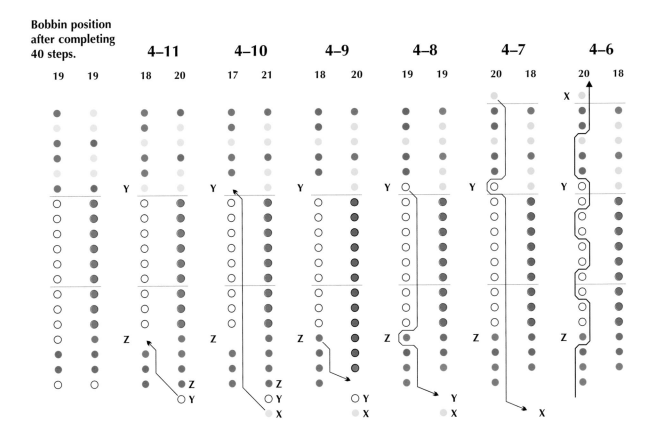

4–11 **4–10** **4–9** **4–8** **4–7** **4–6**

Steps 4–6 to 4–11 show
the left-hand moves.

twill weave with decorative edge

Design 39 shows how to add an edge to a double braid without adding bobbins of another colour. Although only one method is shown here, there are several variations to 'turn' the edges in this way. For example, depressing the last five bobbins on the upper arm instead of three on steps 1 and 3 will give a more generous coloured edge to the design. Two additional ways to turn the edges will be found in designs 40 and 41.

60 bobbins

2 colours:
- 29
- 31

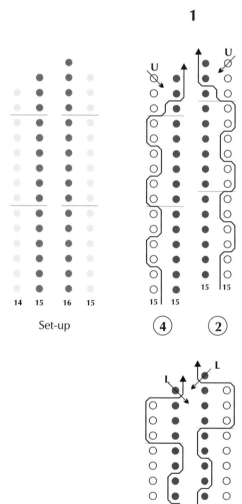

1

14 15 16 15

Set-up

④ ②

15 | 15   15 | 15

③ ①

15 | 16   16 | 15

double braids

All four arms of the takadai are used to make a double braid.
A braid becomes a double braid by making two single braids at the same
time and linking them together as one structure.

The braid on the upper arm of the takadai is usually considered to be the front or right side of the braid. Linking can be at the edges, in the centre of the braid, or by picking up individual stitches to create a pattern. Patterned pick-up braids are explained in chapter 8 (see page 132).

Hand Movements
As with single braids, the hand movements to make double braids are described in a series of steps. The hand moves for double braids are shown differently from single braids. Each step comprises four hand moves, two on the right-hand side and two on the left.

Preparing the Warp
All four single-braid methods of beginning a braid can be used for double braids. When tying the warps to the roller cord make sure that the 'point of braiding' of both braids is lined up one above the other. It is important while braiding to keep the braids advancing at the same pace. If not, the linking of the edges and any exchange of bobbins between levels will be out of line.

Braids linked at both edges make good straps and belts. Those linked on one side only can be used as an edging for clothing, and braids linked in the centre and not the edges can be used to join two pieces of fabric together (far right).

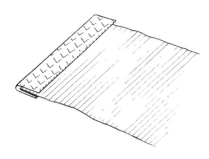

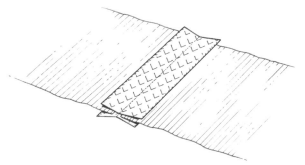

Beating the Warp

Beating a single-braid warp involves two actions: the right hand is used to beat the right-hand side of the braid and the left hand for the left-hand side. Beating double braids on the upper arm remains the same as for single braids, but changes when beating on the lower arm. Beating the shed on the lower arm is made with the opposite hand. Working to the sequence shown below removes the awkwardness of trying to manoeuvre the arm to the correct angle to beat the shed with the same hand on the lower arm.

Move 1: right-hand lower arm – hold the sword in the left hand and beat.
Move 2: right-hand upper arm – hold the sword in the right hand and beat.

Move 3: left-hand lower arm – hold the sword in the right hand and beat.
Move 4: left-hand upper arm – hold the sword in the left hand and beat.

Clamp and Mirror

The mirror is needed so that the underside of the braid can be viewed for possible errors as it is worked. Attach the mirror to the frame on the torii bar, bend the flexible hose and position the mirror so that the underside of the braid is visible.

Finishing the Braid

Choose a finishing technique and secure the warp. Release the bobbins from the takadai, beginning with the bobbins on the upper arm, and then release the bobbins on the lower arm.

NOTE
On the braids on the following pages:
F = Front of braid
B = Back of braid

Here are the setting-up diagram and hand moves for design 40, a plain-weave double braid with 52 bobbins. The step number is shown at the top of the hand moves. There are four hand moves to each step. The lower-arm hand movements are numbered 1 and 3; the upper-arm moves 2 and 4. The hand moves to make a double braid follow this sequence, beginning on the lower right-hand side:

1. Lower right, 2. Upper right, 3. Lower left, 4. Upper left

The braids are linked together at the edges when making steps 2 and 4 on the upper arms.

Note how in the No.1 bobbins are lined up evenly on the koma nearest the braider. This makes it easier to keep track of the correct place.

The letters 'L' and 'U' signify the destination of the weft thread, and these are shown next to the circles pierced by arrows. 'L' indicates that the bobbin is cast to the opposite lower arm, and 'U' to the opposite upper arm.

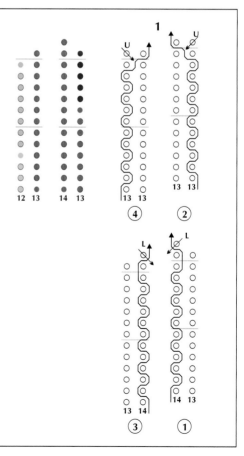

design 40　plain weave

52 bobbins

5 colours:

27 ●
5 ●
8 ●
8 ●
4 ●

Designs 40 and 41 are plain- and twill-weave braids, with multicoloured upper braids and a single-coloured lower braid. The lower braid could also be multicoloured.

Set-up

12　13　　14　13

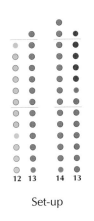

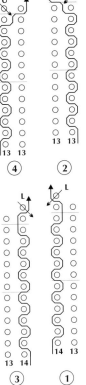

design 41　2/2 twill weave

52 bobbins

7 colours:

28 ●
4 ●
4 ●
5 ●
4 ●
4 ●
4 ●

Set-up

12　13　14　13

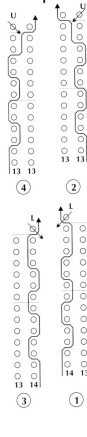

3/3 twill weave

Design 42 is a 3/3 twill braid. Two designs are shown; the two-colour braid shows the basic pattern and the five-colour braid shows how the pattern can be varied when extra colours are added.

2-colour

5-colour

2-colour set-up

5-colour set-up

design 42

46 bobbins

colours:
see set-ups

plain weave – edge reversal

Designs 43 and 44 are plain and twill braids with the edges reversed.

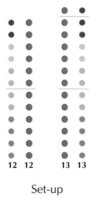

Set-up

design 43

46 bobbins

5 colours:
- 25
- 5
- 4
- 8
- 8

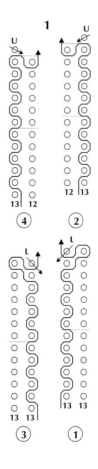

design 44

2/2 twill weave – edge reversal

50 bobbins

7 colours:
25 ●   5 ○
4 ○   4 ○
4 ○   4 ●
4 ●

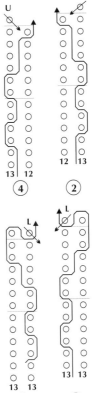

---

design 45

2/2 twill weave – edge reversal

50 bobbins

2 colours:
25 ●
25 ○

Design 45 is a mix of 2/2 and 3/3 twill, a structure that gives a unique pattern to the centre of the braid. This pattern and similar variations are often found wrapped around the hilt of swords for grip and decoration.

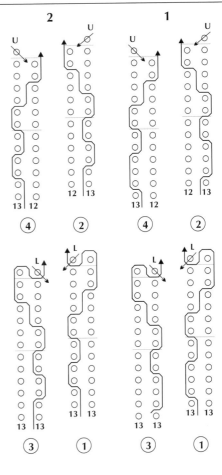

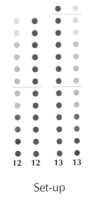

2/2 twill weave – centre linking

Designs 46 and 47 are linked in the centre of the braid, and the edges of design 46 can also be linked. Design 47 is unusual as the two braids are off set.

design 46

50 bobbins

2 colours:
● 25
● 25

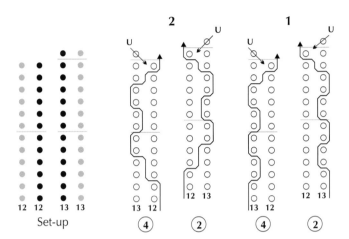

This braid offers three options:

Linked edges only (make the four Step 1 moves)
Linked edges and centre linking (make Step 1 and 2 moves)
Linked centre only (make the four Step 2 moves).

A pattern is created in the centre of the braid by making a length of plain weave, then introducing Step 2 moves at intervals for a predetermined number of steps.

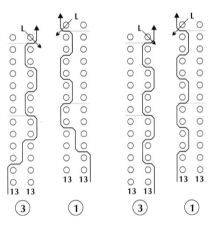

design 47   2/2 twill weave – centre linking

50 bobbins

2 colours:
25 ●
25 ●

This braid is linked in the centre with both sides open at the edge. What is unusual is that the two braids are offset so as to show a little of the underneath braid.

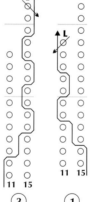

Set-up

Step 1 makes the twill braid without linking.

Step 2 links the braid in the centre.

The combination of the two steps creates the pattern.

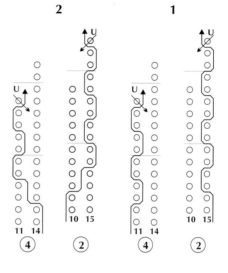

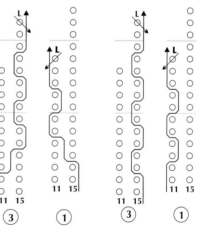

leaf pattern

Designs 48 and 49 are three-dimensional structures showing two very different variations of a leaf pattern. It takes a 24-step cycle to complete one pattern of this braid.

design 48

52 bobbins

2 colours:
● 27
● 25

13 – 24   **7 – 12**   **1 – 6**

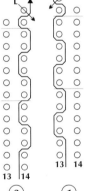

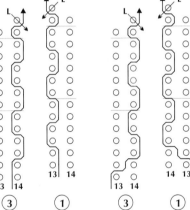

Set-up

Steps 1 to 6:
Hand moves 1 and 3 on the lower arms are made by twill weave, the upper braid moves 2 and 4 are made by plain weave. The two braids are linked together in the centre of the braid when making the twill moves.

Steps 7 to 12:
The hand moves 1 and 3 are made on the lower arms only, there are no steps to be made on the upper arms. The twill structure advances the lower braid ready for the next 12 steps on the upper arm.

Steps 13 to 24:
This unusual hand move will be found later on other designs. There is no shed to open the weft thread is cast in between the upper warp threads and the lower warp to the opposite upper arm.

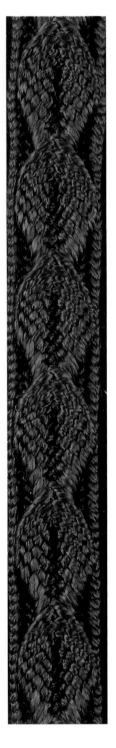

design 49   black-and-white leaf pattern

66 bobbins

2 colours:
33 ●
33 ○

When making the hand moves for steps 13 to 17, note that the weft bobbins are cast in between the upper and lower warps and placed on the opposite upper arms.

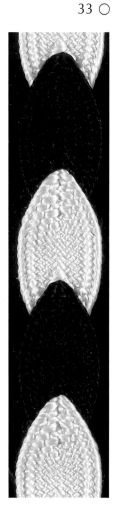

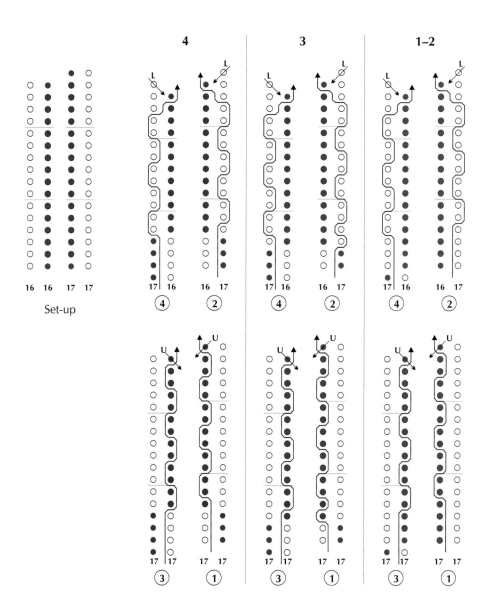

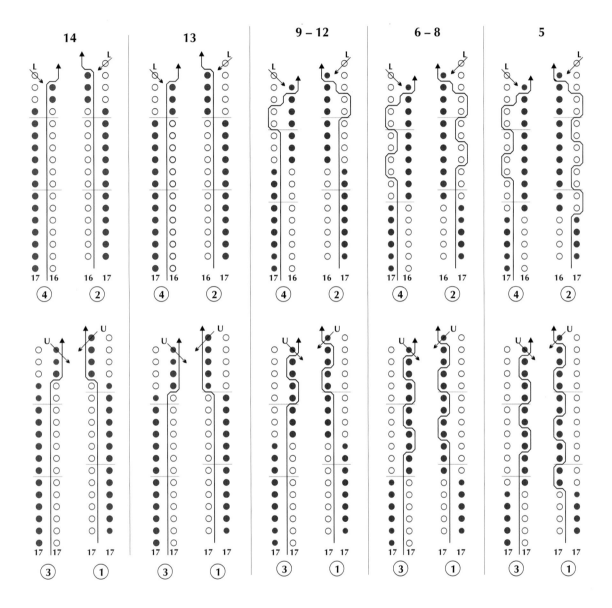

design 49

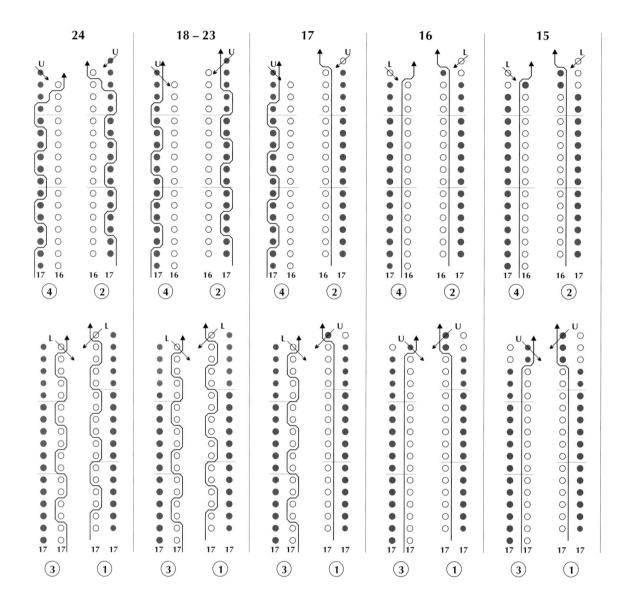

kikko

The kikko (tortoise shell) pattern of design 50 is a symbol of long life. It was a design popular with the samurai as a sword belt.

52 bobbins

colours:
see set-ups

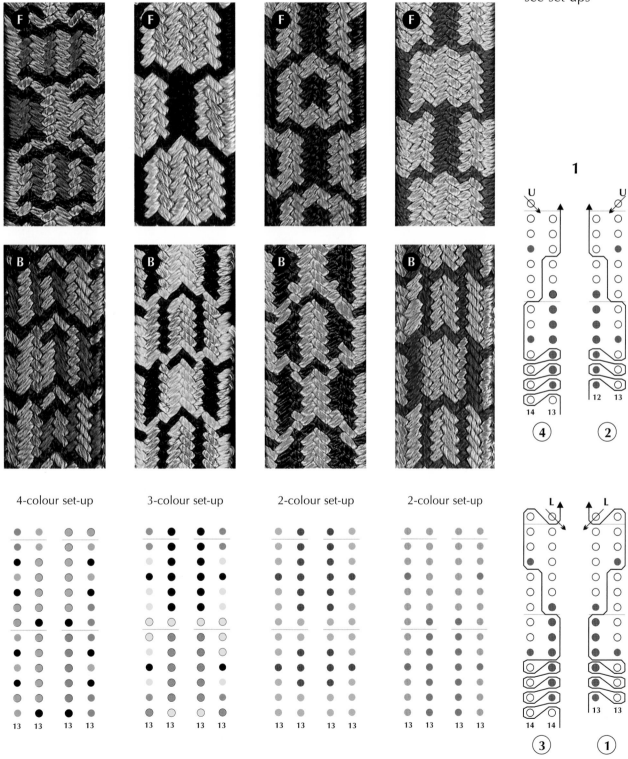

4-colour set-up   3-colour set-up   2-colour set-up   2-colour set-up

design 51   plain and twill weave with centre floats

Bobbins and
colours:
see set-ups

Design 51 – a 40-bobbin plain-weave pattern – shows how this design can be made wider than the traditional 32-bobbin variety. When folded in half lengthways it makes very good edging for garments.

Move 1 and 3:
The bobbins on the lower arm are cast to the opposite upper arm.

Move 2 and 4:
Do not make a shed. Lift the weft bobbin from the upper arm across and over all the upper and lower bobbins placing it on the opposite lower arm.

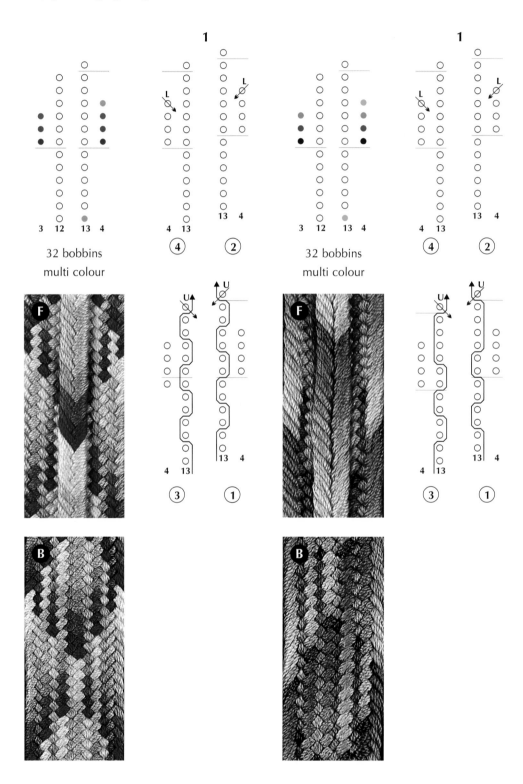

32 bobbins
multi colour

32 bobbins
multi colour

twill weave with links and floats

Design 52 is a variation of design 51. This design was discovered by Hazel Thompson.

1 colour:
● 32

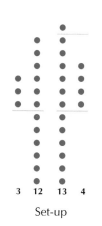

Set-up

3   12   13   4

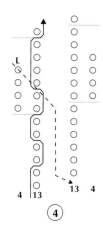

④   4 │13   13   4

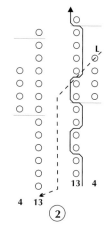

L   4   13   13   4

②

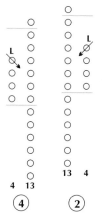

L   4   13   13   4

④   ②

F

Step 1:
Moves 1 to 4 are
the same as those
used in design 41
to make a ridge
down the centre of
the braid.

Step 2:
Moves 1 and 3 are
the same as moves
1 and 3 in Step 1.

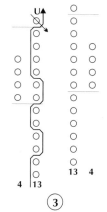

U   4 │13   13   4

③

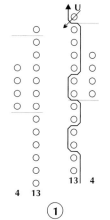

U   4   13   13   4

①

U   4 │13   13   4

③   ①

When the lower bobbin has been cast to the
opposite upper arm, leave the beater in the
shed to keep it open for moves 2 and 4.

Moves 2 and 4: Cast the bobbin from the
upper arm through the shed to the opposite
lower arm and beat the two wefts that now
lie in the same shed.

The design on this page was made by
alternating the pattern every nine steps.

B

design 53   linked layers and floats

46 bobbins

Designs 53 and 54 are two patterns in which a stitch floats over the braid structure giving texture and pattern to the braid.

5 colours:
- 27
- 7
- 4
- 4
- 4

1

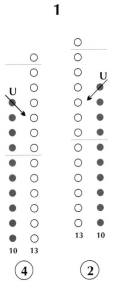

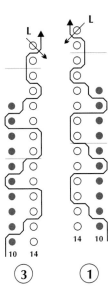

Set-up

9   13   14   10

④   10   13

②   13   10

③   10   14

①   14   10

linked layers and floats

1

40 bobbins

colours:
see set-up

NOTE:
It is recommended
that the coloured
threads that float
over the warp as
the braid is made
are thicker than the
31 one-coloured
bobbins. If they are
the same thickness
they will not cover
and hide the braid
underneath.

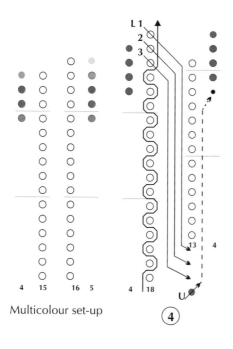

Multicolour set-up

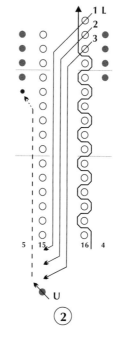

④   ②

Right-hand Moves

Move 1:
Make a shed on the lower arm.

Cast the bobbin from the upper arm
under the upper warps and through the
shed on the lower arm between
bobbins 8 and 10.

Place this bobbin on the lower left-
hand arm, leaving space for the three
lower-arm bobbins.

Cast the three lower bobbins to the
left-hand lower arm.

Move 2:
Move the coloured bobbin from the
lower arm to the left-hand upper arm.

Left-hand Moves

Moves 3 and 4:
Repeat as for the right side, except in
Step 1 the upper bobbin passes
through the lower shed between
bobbins 10 and 12.

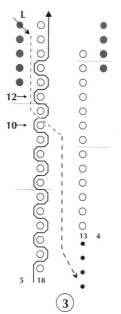

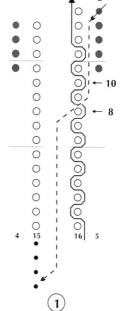

③   ①

pick-up braids

The term 'pick up' means to exchange a thread on the lower braid with one of the opposite colour on the upper braid. Designs created on graph paper determine the point at which exchanges are to be made. When pick-up braids have been mastered, the braider will have reached the highest skill level.

When designing and making pick-up braids it is essential to work systematically to reduce the chance of possible error. A systematic approach is explained by working through a 60-bobbin braid project called the 'Forget-me-not' pattern (see page 142). The project begins by explaining the template on which designs are planned and the hand moves that create the stitches that appear on the surface of the braid. Six diagrammed templates take you through each progressive stage, from planning the Forget-me-not design to the final working instructions.

Takatool and Magnetic Board

The 'takatool' is a guide to help you keep your place in the instructions. It shows the graphed stitches in relation

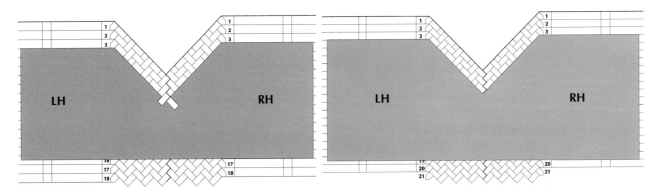

Twill graph for 60-bobbin pick-up braids   *Twill graph for 68-bobbin pick-up braids*

to the weave codes and the stitches that have to be picked up. To make a takatool for the 60- and 68-bobbin designs, use the templates as shown in the Appendix (see page 165). Cut around the outline and use this to make a permanent shape from tinted translucent acetate sheet.

Setting up the takadai

A quick and ordered way to prepare a warp for pick-up braid samples is to begin the warp with a point. It makes the transfer to the takadai from the warping posts much easier. It also facilitates a smooth start when beginning to braid.

Warping for a Pointed End

1. First, prepare two holding cords (one for each colour). Cut two 40in (1m) lengths for each warp using the same yarn as the warp. Begin with the lower dark-coloured warp. Fold the holding cord in half and thread over the first set of warp threads at post B.

2. Continue winding the warp, stopping at intervals to twine around the loops of the warp at post B. When the twining for the lower braids is complete leave the warp on the post.

3. Wind the upper-braid warp on the same posts, following the same procedure as for the lower braid.

4. Push both warps down post B, and pull the holding cords together so they are the same length. Tie all eight ends together with an overhand knot.

5. Cut the warp from post A, transfer it to the takadai and secure the holding cord to the roller cord. Place the upper-braid warp back over the torii. Attach bobbins to the lower warp first, then to the upper warp.

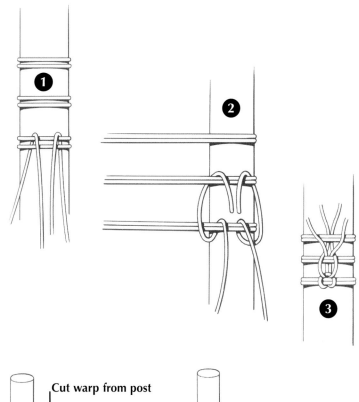

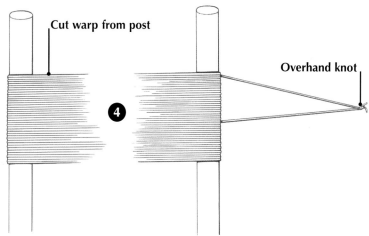

Cut warp from post

Overhand knot

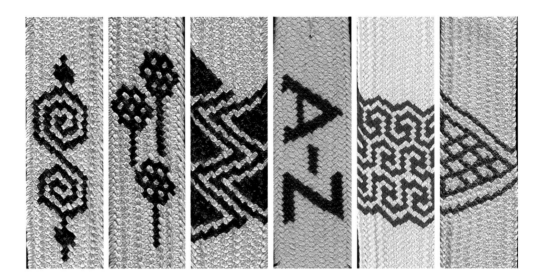

Additional 60 & 68 pick-up patterns

These examples are to be found in the Appendix. They are coded and ready to braid. It is possible to develop each of these patterns. For example, the Alpha braid could become a full alphabet.

planning 60 and 68 double-pattern braids

Kourai Gumi is a Japanese name given to 2/2 twill 'double braids' into which reversible patterns are woven. Most Japanese pick-up braids are made with 60 or 68 bobbins, and are designed around the width of the braid that can be worn as the *obijima* (sash) that is tied over the wide obi. Designs for obijima using fewer bobbins do exist, but are not given here.

Two braids, set up on the upper and lower arms of the takadai, are worked simultaneously in contrasting colours. As the upper and the lower braids are made, the edges are linked together forming a hollow tube. The linked braids remain hollow until the design calls for an exchange of threads between the two levels to create a pattern. The patterns for double braids have to be planned on graph paper before they can be made. This is similar to planning double-woven fabrics like those from Finland and Mexico.

Pattern Stitches

Pattern stitch is the name given to a thread that appears as the opposite colour on the surface of the braid. These stitches are created either by weaving or by exchanging threads between the layers. Designs are planned and drawn on a graph, and a system of codes is used to identify each pattern stitch.

Woven pattern stitches are produced by weaving your hand in and out of the upper and lower warp, making a shed through which a weft thread is passed. Alternatively, exchanging threads vertically between the upper and lower braids creates pick-up pattern stitches.

Making the 'Forget-me-not' Design

The Forget-me-not design that is used in the following exercise is shown on the left. A system of how to plan and code designs is explained opposite, followed by step-by-step instructions on how to draft the Forget-me-not pattern ready for braiding on page 142.

Below: The Forget-me-not design.

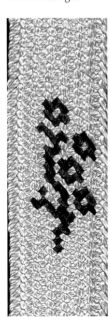

60-bobbin set-up

Cut and prepare a 40in (1m) warp for 60 bobbins, 31 in a dark colour for the lower braid and 29 in a light colour for the upper braid. (A high contrast will ensure that the pattern stitches show clearly.) Arrange the threads on the koma as shown in the set-up diagram.

Note how the No.1 bobbins are lined up evenly on the koma nearest to you. This makes it easier to keep track of where you are. Weaving begins on the right-hand side and, dependent on the coding, opening the shed can begin on either the lower or upper arm. The takadai is now ready for braiding. Before you begin, the following instructions will clarify the pattern graphing and the coding moves.

60-Bobbin Graph Paper

Right is the template on which 60-bobbin double-braid patterns are coded (see Appendix A03 on page 163 for a full-size master template).

The central area of the template shows a graph with 14 vertical columns, with a dark line down the centre separating the right-hand and left-hand sides of the braid. The graph as it appears on the page is a pictorial representation of the upper braid; the lower unseen braid is a mirror image of the upper braid.

The vertical columns of the graph are numbered one to seven, measuring from the centre line to the outside edge of the braid.

Right: Template for 60-bobbin double-braid patterns.

The Coding Columns

On either side of the graph are three coding columns (A, B and C) in which to record the codes that will be given to weave, edge and pick-up stitches. Column D shows the sequential steps to make the braid.

The Graph

Weave stitches for both sides of the braid are indicated on the graph in columns 2, 4 and 6. They move diagonally downwards from the edge of the graph to the centre line. There are eight possible arrangements of weave stitches; each is given a three-letter code. These codes are entered in column A.

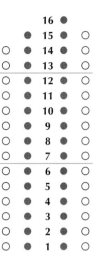

Forget-me-not set-up

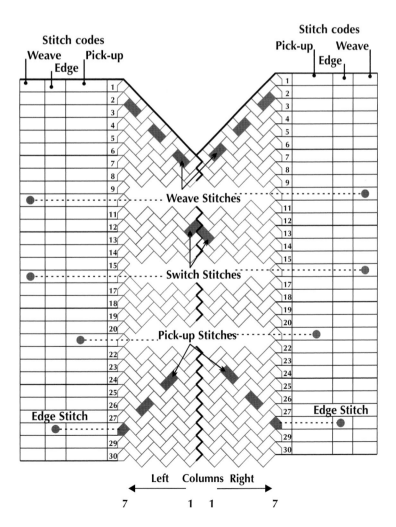

Switch stitches appear only in column 1. They become part of the weave stitch, adding a fourth letter to the weave code. Pick-up stitches move diagonally down from the centre line to the edge of the braid. They appear in the odd numbered columns 3, 5 and 7, and are coded with a number. The edge stitches that appear in column 7 will be given additional letter codes according to the action to be taken.

The instructions of how to code the weave, switch, pick-up and edge stitches are shown below.

Coding the weave stitches

Below: Weave Stitch Hand Movements for 60 Bobbin Braids

Eight Codes Shown below are the eight right-hand and left-hand hand moves used to create weave stitches that fall in columns 2, 4 and 6. Each configuration of hand moves is given a three-letter code. A master set of these hand moves (Fig A09) can be found in the Appendix (see page 169) and used for photocopying.

The code identifies the columns on the graph in which the pattern stitches have been placed, the pathway of the shed, and the destination of the weft. Lower bobbins are cast to the opposite lower arm and the upper bobbins to the upper arm.

The code is comprised of two letters: 'U' (upper) and 'L' (lower). The letter U signifies that a thread from the lower braid will be brought to the surface of the upper braid as a pattern stitch. Consequently, the letter L signifies that a complementary pattern stitch will appear on the lower braid.

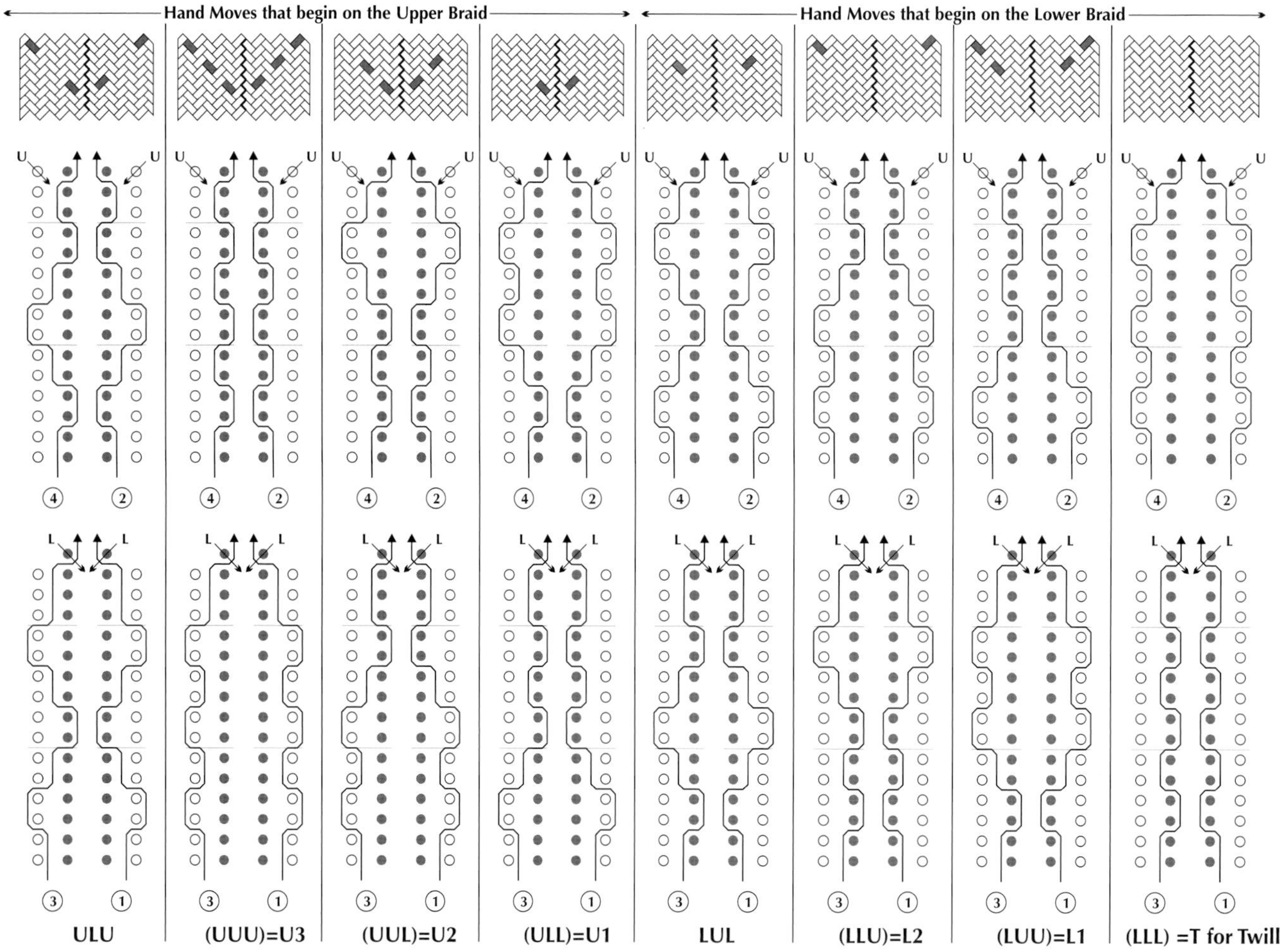

Hand Moves that begin on the Upper Braid				Hand Moves that begin on the Lower Braid			
ULU	(UUU)=U3	(UUL)=U2	(ULL)=U1	LUL	(LLU)=L2	(LUU)=L1	(LLL)=T for Twill

Six of the codes are abbreviated: U1 = ULL, U2 = UUL, U3 = UUU, L1 = LUU, L2 = LLU, and T for Twill = LLL. The codes are shown at the bottom. The letter 'T' has been chosen for twill weave without a pattern stitch being created rather than LLL. This is in keeping with the term for twill used for non-pick-up double-weave patterns in the previous chapters. Codes LUL and ULU are not abbreviated.

To create the pattern stitches shown, the lower bobbins are thrown to the opposite lower arm and the upper bobbins to the opposite upper arm. The weft bobbin to be cast is shown by an arrow at the top of each of the hand moves shown in the diagram. The circled numbers denote the order in which the moves are made.

As musicians practise scales, so should braiders practise codes to transfer the 'knowing' to hands and fingers. It is suggested that before braiding the Forget-me-not pattern you should braid each of the eight codes shown, above right, 24 times, with a plain twill woven section between the codes. This sample will be a permanent reference for the future.

Switch stiches – adding a fourth letter To 'switch' a stitch means to change the destination of the weft. It indicates that when the weft is cast to the opposite side, it goes to the opposite level, placing a lower-level bobbin on the upper arm and an upper-level bobbin on the lower arm. Compare the diagrams A and B (shown right). Diagram B shows an 'S' added to the code. Eventually the switched stitches on the upper braid will have to change position with their partners in the lower braid to prevent their continued appearance as a pattern stitch.

Weave Edge	Pick-up
L1	1
L2	2
LUL	3
U1	4
U2	5
U3	6
ULU	7
T	8
T	9
T	10
T	11

Pick-up Edge	Weave
1	L1
2	L2
3	LUL
4	U1
5	U2
6	U3
7	ULU
8	T
9	T
10	T
11	T

Plotting the codes
This graph shows how the eight-coded weave stitches are entered on both sides of the graph. The pattern as it appears here is asymmetrical – the right-hand side is slightly higher than the left.

NOTE:
Weave stitches always point towards the centre of the braid.

Switch Stitches
When a weave stitch crosses over the centre line and falls in column 1 on the opposite side, as shown above, the letter 'S' for switch is added to the code.

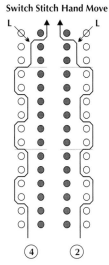

B
Switch Stitch Hand Move

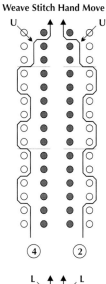

A
Weave Stitch Hand Move

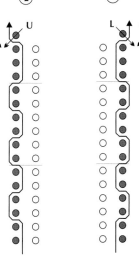

Picking up and exchanging bobbins.

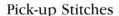

Pick-up Stitches

Pick-up exchanges between the upper and lower braids are always made prior to opening a shed and casting a weft bobbin. A bobbin is 'picked up' when a design calls for a pattern stitch to appear in a designated position, and it is 'put back' when it is no longer required to appear. Pick-up stitches fall in the odd-numbered columns 1, 3 and 5. (The method is shown above.)

How to Change Pick-up Bobbins

The exchange of bobbins takes place between 'pairs' of bobbins that are in the same position on the upper and lower arms (i.e. a No.3 upper bobbin must exchange with a No.3 lower bobbin). The pairs will always be of opposite colours in a two-coloured braid. When the pick-up bobbins have been exchanged, make sure that the correct bobbins have been selected by checking the colour arrangement. A common mistake is to pick up an adjacent bobbin in error.

The process of picking up (exchanging) a pair of bobbins between the upper and lower arms is shown above. First identify the pair of bobbins to be exchanged, Step **(1)** shows the right-hand No.3 bobbins to be changed.

While pressing down, pull the upper and lower No.1 and No.2 bobbin threads towards you to reveal the No.3 bobbin on both levels **(1)**. Lift up No.3 bobbin from the lower arm and place the thread in front of No.3 bobbin on the upper arm **(2)**. The procedure is the same for the left hand.

Lift the upper bobbin over the lower bobbin, placing it down to its new position on the lower arm, as shown in Figs **(3)** and **(4)**. The No.3 bobbins have now changed places, and the exchange is complete.

When a design calls for a number of bobbins to be exchanged – for example, bobbins 3, 4 and 5 in one move – always begin with lowest bobbin number and work towards the highest number. Pull the pairs of threads that have already been exchanged towards you to access the next pair to be worked.

Correcting Mistakes When a mistake is discovered, and there will be mistakes, do not panic and start randomly undoing sheds or pick-ups. The mistake is likely to have occurred several moves back, so it is important to discern exactly where you are and work backwards one step at a time.

The work has to be unbraided, reversing the whole process, and the sheds for the upper and lower levels are opened and the weft bobbin taken back. Then the picked-up pairs are exchanged, taking care to rotate the bobbins in the opposite direction, returning them to their original position. This is crucial, as you can easily end up with twisted threads.

Identify the 'Key' Bobbins Looking down at the upper braid on the takadai, examine the structure and compare it with the illustration below left. As the braid forms, each of the warps is at one of four positions in the structure: under two, over one, over two, and under one.

The bobbins that have covered two wefts are ready to be to be picked up and exchanged with their partners on the lower braid. These bobbins are known as the 'key' bobbins.

The key bobbins will always occupy positions 3, 7, 11 and 15 in the warp. This is further explained in the illustration below right.

Which Bobbins can be Exchanged?
The key bobbins 3, 7 and 11 are at the last point in the structure (over two) where an exchange between the upper

NOTE:
'Pairs' are the threads that appear in the same position on the upper and lower arms (e.g. No.3 upper and No.3 lower). The pairs will always be of opposite colours in a two-coloured braid.

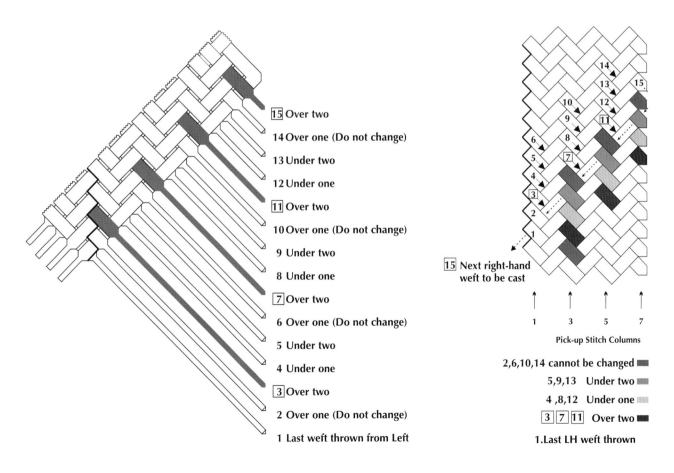

15 Over two

14 Over one (Do not change)

13 Under two

12 Under one

11 Over two

10 Over one (Do not change)

9 Under two

8 Under one

7 Over two

6 Over one (Do not change)

5 Under two

4 Under one

3 Over two

2 Over one (Do not change)

1 Last weft thrown from Left

15 Next right-hand weft to be cast

Pick-up Stitch Columns

2,6,10,14 cannot be changed ▪
5,9,13 Under two ▪
4 ,8,12 Under one ▪
3 7 11 Over two ▪

1.Last LH weft thrown

and lower bobbins may take place. All pick-ups could be exchanged at these key bobbin points. However, it is more economical to exchange two or three bobbins at one time. The illustration shows that bobbins 4, 5, 8, 9, 12 and 13 can also be exchanged at the same time as the key bobbins.

Remember that all the pick-ups have to exchange prior to making a shed and casting the weft.

The black arrows show the stitches disappearing under the wefts. Bobbins 2, 6, 10 and 14 cannot be exchanged as they have only passed over one weft thread. Bobbin 1 was the last weft thrown from the left-hand side.

The next step is to identify and code the pick-up stitches using an arrowhead and number.

Coding the pick-up stitches

Adding the Arrowheads Pick-up stitches appear in columns 1, 3 and 5. They move diagonally down the graph from the centre line to the edge of the braid. All the stitches must be identified and marked with an arrowhead before

giving a stitch a numerical code. Place an arrowhead at the bottom of the stitch pointing in the direction it is travelling to indicate that it has to be exchanged at this point; either to stop an existing pattern stitch from continuing into the next column, or to create a new pattern stitch.

Letters have been used in chart **(1)** below to explain why these stitches have been identified and need to be exchanged. All the letters will be replaced by bobbin numbers, as shown in chart **(2)**.

The seven pattern stitches shown in column 1 were created by switch stitches, thrown from the left-hand side of the braid. Those marked 'F' will not continue as pattern stitches and must be returned to their original position. After the pattern is coded with arrowheads the next step is to add the pick-up number.

Entering the Pick-up Number Codes Always begin at the bottom of the graph, starting with column 1 on the right-hand side, and work upwards.

A = Add a new pattern stitch.

F = Finished. This pattern stitch will stop at this point and will not reappear as a pattern stitch.

C = Continue. Allows a pattern stitch to continue into the next column.

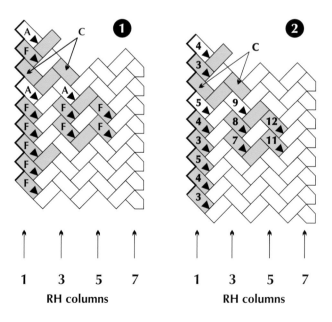

The first pattern stitch in column number 1 is given the number 3. (Remember: the key bobbins are 3, 7 and 11.) Work up the column identifying stitches in groups of three wherever possible. Each design presents a different situation.

Continue on to work column number 3 beginning with key bobbin 7, then column number 5 with key bobbin 11. Complete the right-hand side before starting on the left-hand side and repeating the process. Finally, enter the number codes in the column on the graph next to the weave stitch codes, see chart (3).

Transfer Codes to the Pick-up Column When transferring the numbers from the graph to the pick-up code column the number should be identified as to whether it is a pattern stitch returning to the lower arm or a new stitch being created. Returning pattern stitches are shown inside a circle; for example, at step 7 the number three is shown like this. New pattern stitches are shown without a circle; for example, at step 7 the number 4.

When the pick-up code numbers are entered in the pick-up column, braiding can commence. To ensure that the pick-up numbers on the graph are placed on the correct line in the pick-up column, use the takatool.

Starting at column 1, align the takatool with the column and the step on which the number is to be placed. Work up the graph, systematically transferring the numbers one column at a time to the pick-up column (4).

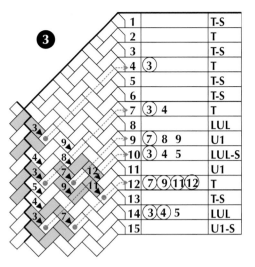

1		T-S
2		T
3		T-S
4	(3)	T
5		T-S
6		T-S
7	(3) 4	T
8		LUL
9	(7) 8 9	U1
10	(3) 4 5	LUL-S
11		U1
12	(7)(9)(11)(12)	T
13		T-S
14	(3)(4) 5	LUL
15		U1-S

Left: To ensure that the pick-up numbers on the graph are placed on the correct line in the pick-up column, use the takatool.

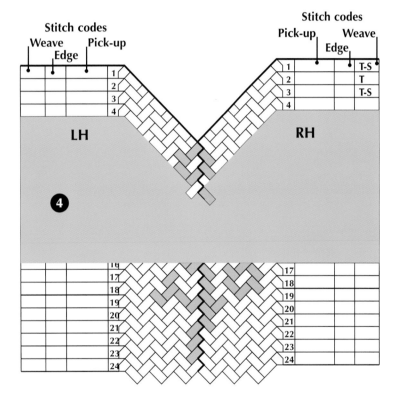

Drafting a complete design

To support the learning on the previous pages, copy the Forget-me-not pattern **(1)** onto a blank master template. Follow and complete each of the five steps below through to the completed draft (overleaf).

1 **Colour in the Pattern and Code the Weave Stitches**. Using a soft graphite pencil rather than felt-markers, lightly shade in the Forget-me-not pattern onto your full-page graph.

2 **Using the Takatool** Mask the pattern with the takatool. Work by sliding the takatool down the page one line at a time. Code all the weave stitches on the right-hand side before coding the left-hand side, then check the results using diagram **(2)**.

3 **Enter Weave Codes** Figure **(2)** shows the weave codes inserted. The next step is to enter the arrowheads for the pick-up stitches.

4 **Entering the Arrowheads** Start on the right-hand side at step 1 and work down the page, placing an arrowhead on each of the stitches that have to be exchanged **(3)**. Repeat this process on the left-hand side.

The arrows on the white stitches mark the new pattern stitches to be added. Arrows on the coloured pattern stitches indicate that they are to be returned to the lower level. The next step is to give each arrow a code number to indicate which bobbins have to be exchanged **(4)**.

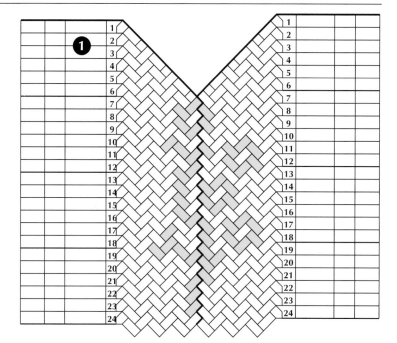

5 Number the Pick-up Stitches

Begin the coding on the right-hand side at the bottom of column 1 and then work upwards, grouping the pick-up bobbins in threes wherever it is possible.

Following up column 1, notice that the first six stitches in column 1 run consecutively, therefore two groups of 3, 4, 5 can be picked-up together. This is followed by a gap, then another group of three. The next two stitches are numbered 3 and 4 followed by another gap and one stitch by itself numbered 3.

Column 3 starts with a group of 7, 8 and 9 followed by a gap. The next two stitches 7 and 9 are grouped together as if they were a group of three. The column ends with another group of 7, 8 and 9.

6 Transfer Codes to Pick-up Column

Move the numbers from the grid to the pick-up columns, as shown in (5). Begin on the right-hand side of the graph, by placing the takatool at the bottom of the graph. Work up each column starting with column 1, separately transferring the stitch numbers to the pick-up column.

Place the numbers on the line where they are to be exchanged, remembering to place a circle around a number when it is an existing pattern stitch that has to be returned to the lower level. A plain number is used for a pattern stitch that is being created.

Before going on to edge stitches, try working the patterns without edge stitches as shown in the Appendix (see page 160).

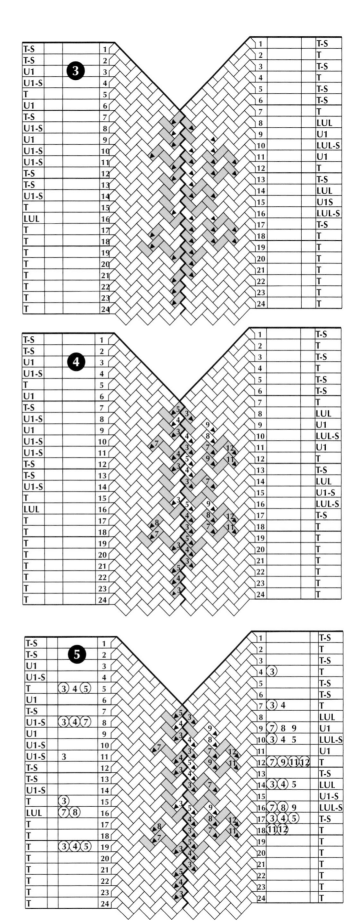

The following shows the Forget-me-not design pattern chart.

Left chart:

Move	Circled	Row
T-S		1
T-S		2
ULL		3
ULL-S		4
T	(3) 4 (5)	5
ULL		6
T-S		7
ULL-S	(3)(4)(7)	8
ULL		9
ULL-S		10
ULL-S	3	11
T-S		12
T-S		13
ULL-S		14
T	(3)	15
LUL	(7)(8)	16
T		17
T		18
T	(3)(4)(5)	19
T		20
T		21
T		22
T		23
T		24
		25
		26
		27
		28
		29
		30
		31
		32
		33
		34
		35
		36

Right chart:

Row	Circled	Move
1		T-S
2		T
3		T-S
4	(3)	T
5		T-S
6		T-S
7	(3) 4	T
8		LUL
9	(7) 8 9	ULL
10	(3) 4 5	LUL-S
11		ULL
12	(7)(9)(11)(12)	T
13		T-S
14	(3)(4) 5	LUL
15		ULL-S
16	(7)(8) 9	LUL-S
17	(3)(4)(5)	T-S
18	(11)(12)	T
19		T
20		T
21		T
22		T
23		T
24		T
25		
26		
27		
28		
29		
30		
31		
32		
33		
34		
35		
36		

The Forget-me-not design pattern.

Coding Edge Stitches

The instructions so far have shown how to remove pattern stitches to prevent them appearing in column seven on the edge of the braid. This section shows how to plan to include edge stitches as part of your design, by allowing previously created pattern stitches to run onto the edge of the braid or planning to pick-up a stitch in column five to appear on the edge in column seven.

Three codes – LL, UU and R – are used in conjunction with the weave codes. LL (lower/lower) and UU (upper/upper) determine which bobbins are to be cast through as weft bobbins; R changes (reverses) the designated weave codes. To get a better understanding of these new codes, set up a warp, follow the directions given below and work through the examples shown.

Codes LL and UU When a pattern stitch on the upper arm reaches the bobbin No.15 position, it will be the same dark colour as bobbin No.16 on the lower arm, making it impossible to cast a light-coloured bobbin from the upper arm. It is when this position is reached that two opposite-coloured bobbins have to be cast from the lower arm, and the code LL is added to the weave code.

The code LL indicates that two bobbins are to be cast from the lower arm as wefts. The first bobbin thrown is identified as if it were the usual bobbin from the lower arm, and the second bobbin as if it were being thrown from the upper arm. The destination of the bobbins is still determined by the weave code given to the pattern that appears on the graph. The same applies to the code UU.

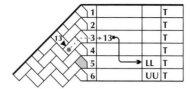

Bobbin No.13 is picked up at Step 3. This stitch travels under two wefts to appear as pattern stitch on the edge of the braid at Step 5. It is at Step 5 that the code LL is introduced, and is then followed by code UU on Step 6.

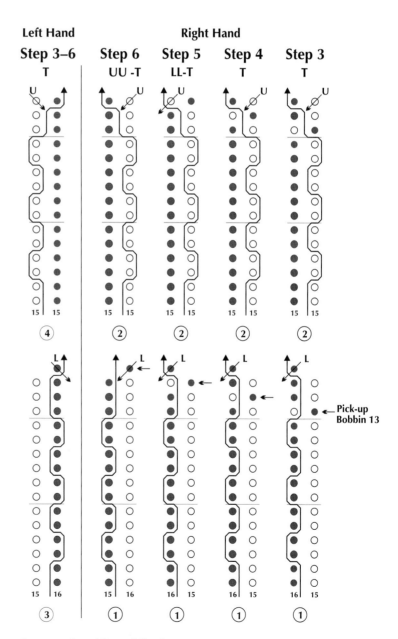

For steps 1 and 2 see following page.

The first of the two bobbins on the upper arm is cast through the shed as if it were a bobbin from the lower arm, and the second bobbin as if coming from the upper arm.

At Step 5 (move 1) the dark bobbin No.15 on the upper arm has reached the last upper bobbin position. It is the same colour as bobbin No.16 on the lower arm, making it impossible to cast wefts of the opposite colour.

Because there are a greater number of bobbins on the lower arm, two bobbins are cast from this level (LL), the dark thread to the lower left arm and the light to the upper left arm.

Step 6 (move 1) shows that again the two end bobbins are the same colour and that there are now 16 bobbins on the upper arm and 15 on the lower arm. Now the upper arm has the greater number of bobbins, two bobbins are cast from this level (UU). The dark exchanged bobbin on the upper arm goes to the lower left and the light colour to the upper left, completing the sequence of moves.

Code R When two or more edge stitches appear consecutively on the edge of the braid, the code R (reversal) always follows an LL code. After casting the two lower LL wefts the structure of the braid will be reversed. There will be 16 bobbins on the upper arm and 14 on the lower arm. Bobbin 16 on the upper arm will be a dark colour and bobbin 14 on the lower arm will be light. The weave codes for this are shown on the facing page. The hand moves for code-R steps are different from the hand moves used for non-edge stitch braids.

A Question of Linking When making a braid without edge stitches

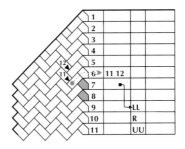

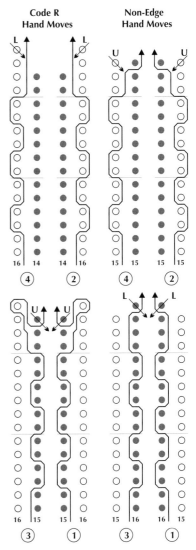

NOTE:

It is the 2nd bobbin cast in the LL and UU moves in steps 5 and 6 that links the braids together.

the linking together of the upper and lower braids happens when casting a bobbin from the upper arm.

What is Normal for Non-edge Steps? By comparing the hand moves shown above, it will become apparent that the normal destination of the bobbins for the non-edge hand moves sends the weft from the lower arm to lower arm and upper to upper. Therefore no pattern stitch appears on the upper braid. It is the switch stitch that creates a pattern stitch, as the lower weft goes to the upper and upper to lower.

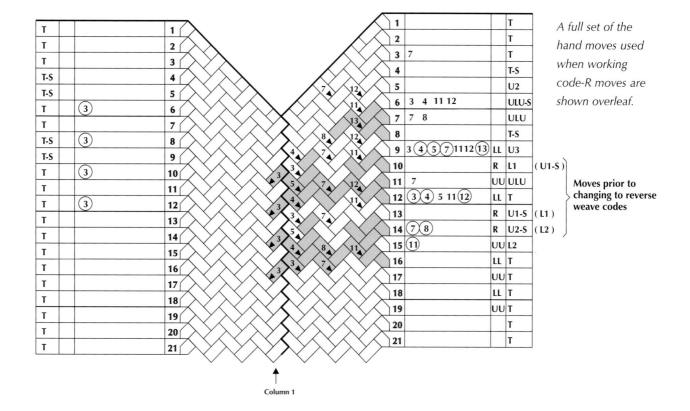

A full set of the hand moves used when working code-R moves are shown overleaf.

Column 1

Moves prior to changing to reverse weave codes

What is Normal for Code-R steps?

The normal hand move for code-R steps is to switch the wefts. A light-coloured bobbin on the lower arm is cast to the upper arm, and a dark bobbin on the upper arm to the lower arm. Therefore no pattern appears on the upper braid.

When a pattern stitch is required to appear on the upper braid in a code-R step, the light-colour wefts on the lower arm are cast to the opposite lower arm and the dark colour on the upper arm to the opposite upper arm. (This can be verified by checking to see if a pattern stitch appears on the graph in column 1 on the opposite side.)

Inverting the Code-R Weave Codes

For each step where a code R is to be made, the weave code and the bobbin's destination has to be inverted (reversed). This is decided by looking at the pattern on the graph. For example, Step 14 shows the pattern on the graph reading as a L2 step. As there is no pattern (switch) stitch appearing on the opposite side of the braid in column 1 of the graph, the weave code inverts to a U2-S. In Step 10, the pattern on the graph shows a pattern stitch appearing in column 1 on the opposite side as a U1-S step, so this inverts to read L1.

To understand the process of dealing with code-R steps, work through the pattern above, at the same time as following the detailed hand moves given on the following page.

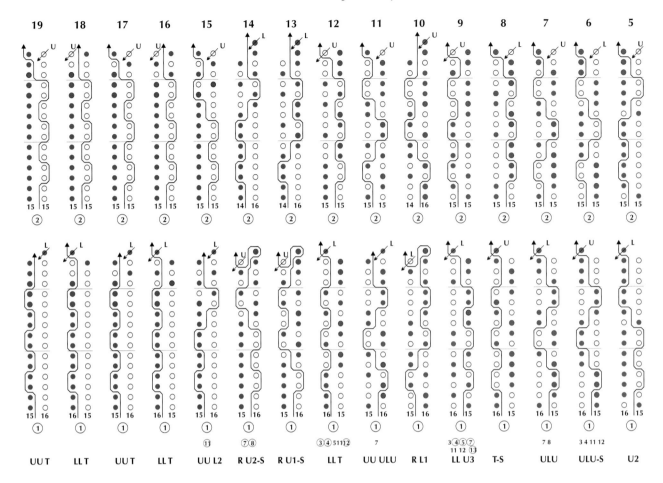

Steps 10, 13 and 14 show two sets of weave codes. The bracketed codes represent the pattern plotted on the graph. These codes would apply if the greater number of bobbins were on the lower arm. However, because the braid at these steps is now, as it were, upside-down with the greater number of bobbins on the upper arm, the codes have to be inverted and coded opposite to the plotted pattern. The corrected codes are shown inside the weave-code column. The hand moves are shown on the facing page.

Destination of the Weft Bobbins

The hand moves for three reversal stitches at steps 10, 13 and 14 are shown opposite. Step 10 calls for a pattern stitch to appear on the left-hand side in column 1, whereas steps 13 and 14 do not.

At Step 10, the lower bobbin is a light colour and is cast to the lower level and the upper dark to the upper level. However, in steps 14 and 15 a pattern stitch is not required to appear in column 1 on the left-hand side and these two moves are thrown as switch stitches.

POINTS TO REMEMBER FOR PROCESSING EDGE STITCHES:

Confirm the move you are about to make is correct by checking the weave codes with the stitches that are plotted on the graph.

When there is only one pattern stitch formed on the edge of the braid, an LL code is immediately followed on the next step by a UU code.

When there are two or more pattern stitches together on the edge of the braid, the LL code is followed on the next step by code R.

When the code R is introduced it inverts the weave code that is plotted on the graph.

The last code R is always followed by the UU code.

Code-R hand moves that do not require a pattern stitch to appear in column 1 on the opposite side of the graph are always switch stitches.

Below: RH & LH reversal hand moves for 60 bobbin braids.

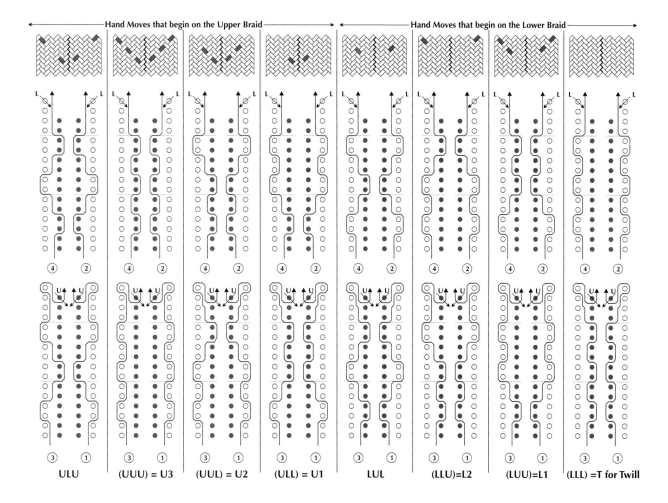

ULU   (UUU) = U3   (UUL) = U2   (ULL) = U1   LUL   (LLU)=L2   (LUU)=L1   (LLL) =T for Twill

Left hand-moves table (steps 1–36):

Code	Code 2	Numbers	Step
T			1
T			2
T-S			3
T-S			4
T			5
U1		3 (4) 5	6
U1			7
LUL		(7)	8
U2-S		(3)	9
U1-S			10
LUL		7 (8) 9	11
U2-S		3	12
ULU-S		(11)	13
L1			14
LUL-S			15
ULU-S		3 (4) 5 (7) 8 (9)	16
U1			17
L1			18
U3	LL	(11) 13	19
U1	UU	(7) (9)	20
U1	LL		21
T	UU		22
T			23
LUL			24
LUL			25
LUL		7 8	26
T		11 12 13	27
T			28
L2	LL		29
U2-S	R		30
U2-S	R		31
U3-S	R		32
U3-S	R		33
U3-S	R		34
T	UU		35
T			36

Right hand-moves table (steps 1–36):

Step	Numbers	Code 2	Code
1			T
2			T
3			T-S
4	3 4		T
5	7		T
6			LUL
7	1112		L2-S
8	3 (4) (7) 8) 9		U2-S
9			U1
10		LL	LUL
11	7 (8) 11(12)	R	T-S
12	(3) 4 5	UU	L2
13		LL	U1-S
14	(7)	UU	L2
15	(3) 4 (11)12 13	LL	T
16		UU	L1
17	(7) 8	LL	U1
18		R	ULU
19	(3) (4) 5 (11)1213	UU	U1
20		LL	T
21	(7)(8) 9	R	U2-S
22		R	U3-S
23	(11)(12) 13	UU	L2
24		LL	T
25		R	U3-S
26		UU	T
27			T
28			T
29			T
30			T
31			T
32			T
33			T
34			T
35			T
36			T

Above: The hand moves for the snowbush design.

Snowbush Design

The snowbush design is coded and ready for braiding. It includes several edge-stitch variations to practise before going on to design your own patterns. To help understand the process of working with edge stitches, a complete set of the hand moves from Step 10 through to Step 36 are shown below, followed by a full set of hand moves for the code-R moves.

Step 16	Step 15	Step 14	Step 13	Step 12	Step 11	Step 10
LH RH	LH RH	LH RH	LH RH	LH RH	LH RH	LH RH

Step 16: 15 15 15 15 / 4 2 ; 15 16 15 16 / 3 1 ; ULU-S ③④5⑦⑧⑨ UU-L1

Step 15: 15 15 15 15 / 4 2 ; 15 16 16 15 / 3 1 ; LUL-S ③4⑪12 13 LL-T

Step 14: 15 15 15 15 / 4 2 ; 15 16 16 15 / 3 1 ; L1 ⑦ UU-L2

Step 13: 15 15 15 15 / 4 2 ; 15 16 16 15 / 3 1 ; ⑪ ULU-S

Step 12: 15 15 15 15 / 4 2 ; 15 16 15 16 / 3 1 ; U2-S 3 ③45 UU-L2 7⑧9

Step 11: 15 14 16 / 4 2 ; 15 16 15 16 / 3 1 ; LUL 7⑧9 (R)-TS 7⑧11⑫

Step 10: 15 15 16 15 / 4 2 ; 15 16 16 15 / 3 1 ; U1-S LL-LUL

Step 23	Step 22	Step 21	Step 20	Step 19	Step 18	Step 17
LH RH	LH RH	LH RH	LH RH	LH RH	LH RH	LH RH

Step 23: 15 15 15 15 / 4 2 ; 15 16 15 16 / 3 1 ; T UU-L2 ⑪⑫13

Step 22: 15 15 14 16 / 4 2 ; 16 15 15 16 / 3 1 ; UU-T (R)-U3S

Step 21: 15 15 15 15 / 4 2 ; 15 16 15 16 / 3 1 ; LL-U1 (R)-U2S ⑦⑧9

Step 20: 15 15 15 15 / 4 2 ; 16 15 16 15 / 3 1 ; UU-U1 ⑦⑨ LL-T

Step 19: 15 15 15 15 / 4 2 ; 15 16 15 16 / 3 1 ; LL-U3 ⑪13 UU-U1 ③④5⑪12 13

Step 18: 15 15 14 16 / 4 2 ; 15 15 15 15 / 3 1 ; L1 (R)-ULU

Step 17: 15 15 15 15 / 4 2 ; 16 15 16 15 / 3 1 ; U1 LL-U1 ⑦8

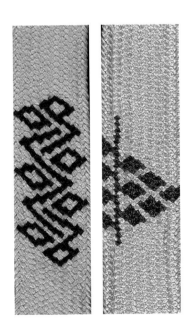

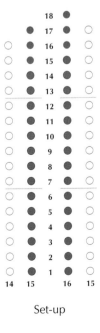

planning 68-bobbin double-pattern braids

Coding and making 68-bobbin braids follows roughly the same procedure as 60-bobbin braids, although there are several differences. The differences will be best understood by working through the two fully coded designs that have been prepared, and by reading the explanations that follow.

Making Two Designs

Cut and prepare a 39in (1m) warp and set this up to make the two designs shown right. The instructions to make these designs are given below. Arrange the 68 bobbins on the four arms, with 35 dark colour threads on the lower arms and 33 light colour threads on the upper arms (see set-up diagram).

Set-up

68-Bobbin Graph Paper

The differences between 60- and 68-bobbin graph paper can be seen by comparing the two graphs. Two columns have been added to the centre of the 68-bobbin graph. There are 16 vertical columns in the graph with the weave stitches falling in columns 1, 3, 5 and 7.

Note how the stitches in the centre columns angle upwards from the centre to the edge, thereby making them part of the weave code. They are not created by switch stitches as they were in the 60-bobbin graph. Switch stitches will appear in column 2 (grey circle).

The template on which to plan and code 68-bobbin designs shows placement of the weave, pick-up and edge stitches on the graph. The weave stitches appear in columns 1, 3, 5 and 7. Switch stitches are located in column 2 and are part of the weave code when used. Pick-up stitches are selected in columns 2, 4 and 6, and the edge stitches falling into column 8 are given the additional code R when in use.

68-Bobbin Weave Stitches

The 16 weave codes with hand moves are shown in two groups. Group 1 displays eight hand-move codes that begin on the lower arm. Note that these hand moves begin with two bobbins being lifted up on the back of the hand. All the codes describe the hand moves with four letters and, as with the 60-bobbin codes, four are abbreviated: LLLL = T for Twill, LUUU = L1, LLUU = L2, and LLLU = L3.

Group 2 displays eight hand-move codes that begin on the upper arm. The hand moves begin with the first two bobbins being pressed down. There are four abbreviations: ULLL = U1, UULL = U2, UUUL = U3, and UUUU = U4.

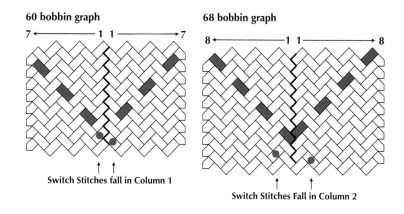

60 bobbin graph

68 bobbin graph

Switch Stitches fall in Column 1

Switch Stitches Fall in Column 2

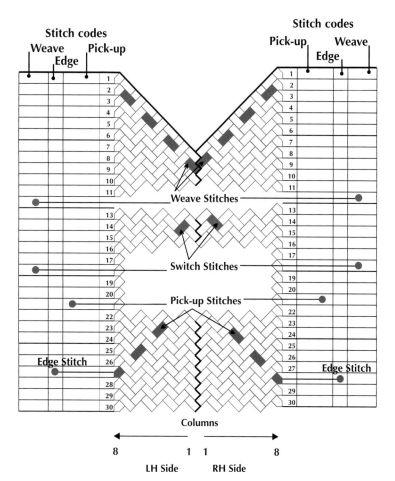

Above: the template on which to plan and code 68-bobbin designs.

RH & LH Weave Stitch Hand Moves for 68 Bobbin Braids that begin on the Lower Braid

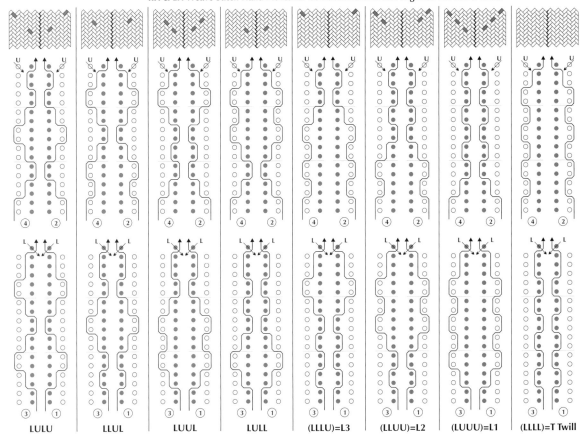

LULU   LLUL   LUUL   LULL   (LLLU)=L3   (LLUU)=L2   (LUUU)=L1   (LLLL)=T Twill

RH & LH Weave Stitch Hand Moves for 68 Bobbin Braids that begin on the Upper Braid

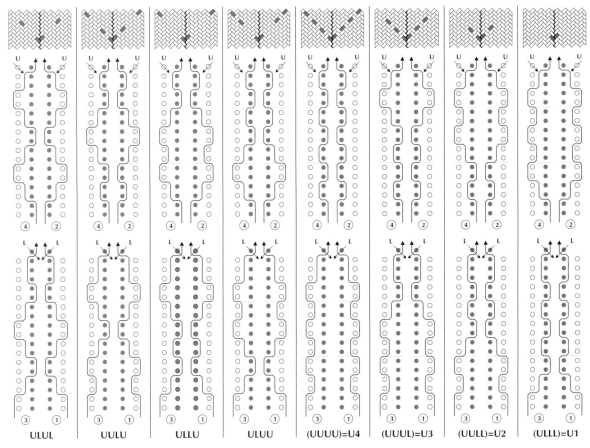

ULUL   UULU   ULLU   ULUU   (UUUU)=U4   (UUUL)=U3   (UULL)=U2   (ULLL)=U1

The weft bobbin to be cast is indicated by an arrow. To create pattern stitches shown on the graphs on page 154, the lower bobbins are thrown to the opposite lower arm, and the upper bobbins to the opposite upper arm. A master set of these hand moves can be found in the Appendix (see page 170–171).

Plotting the Weave Codes

With the memory of the 60 bobbins still imbedded in your hands, they will need to be re-educated to the 68-bobbin hand moves. It is suggested that these codes are practised thoroughly, making 24 repeats of each code until the new moves come naturally.

Switch Stitches – Adding the Letter 'S'

When a weave stitch is planned to cross over the centre line and falls in column 2 on the opposite side (as shown, right), the letter 'S' (standing for 'switch') is added to the code. To switch a stitch means changing the destination of the weft. It indicates that the weft has to be cast not only to the opposite side, but also to the opposite level, placing a lower-level bobbin on the upper arm and an upper-level bobbin on the lower arm.

Eventually all switched stitches appearing on the upper braid will have to change position with their partners in the lower braid to prevent their continued appearance as pattern stitches.

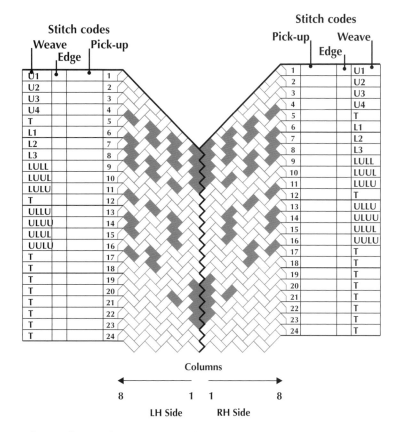

Above: all 16 codes plotted onto the graph. Practise braiding these codes before going on to make the designs that follow.

Right: switch stitches — adding the letter 'S'.

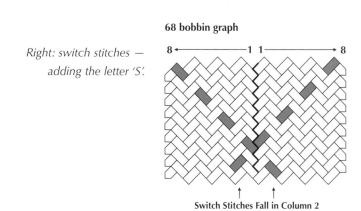

68 bobbin graph

Switch Stitches Fall in Column 2

Pick-up Codes and Key Bobbins

Note that the pick-up codes have changed because the key-bobbin positions have changed. A change in structure occurs whenever an additional eight bobbins are added to the braid. As the extra bobbins are added to the front of the set-up arrangement, the key bobbins move up two places from their 60-bobbin braid position.

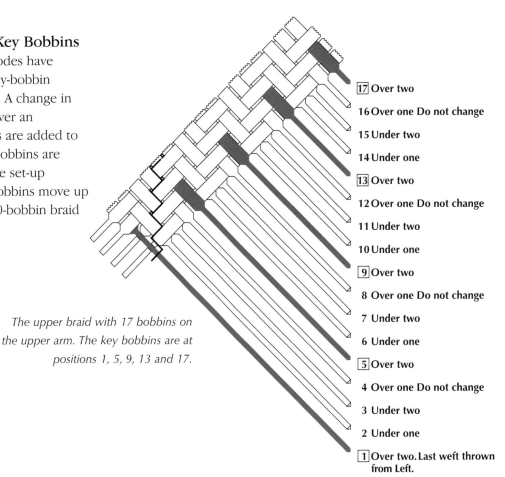

17 Over two

16 Over one Do not change

15 Under two

14 Under one

13 Over two

12 Over one Do not change

11 Under two

10 Under one

9 Over two

8 Over one Do not change

7 Under two

6 Under one

5 Over two

4 Over one Do not change

3 Under two

2 Under one

1 Over two. Last weft thrown from Left.

The upper braid with 17 bobbins on the upper arm. The key bobbins are at positions 1, 5, 9, 13 and 17.

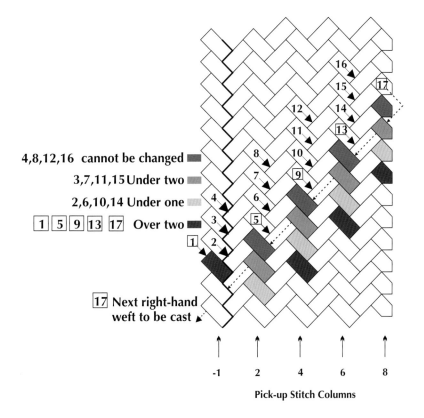

4,8,12,16 cannot be changed

3,7,11,15 Under two

2,6,10,14 Under one

1 5 9 13 17 Over two

17 Next right-hand weft to be cast

-1 2 4 6 8

Pick-up Stitch Columns

Which Bobbins Can Be Exchanged?

The key bobbins 1, 5, 9 and 13 are at the last position in the structure where a pick up can take place. The bobbins 2, 3, 6, 7, 10, 11, 14 and 15 can also be exchanged at the same time as the key bobbins (see graph, left).

Bobbins 4, 8, 12 and 16 cannot be exchanged as they have only passed over one weft thread. Bobbin No.1 is the last weft thrown from the left-hand side and bobbin No.17 is the next weft waiting to be cast from the right-hand side.

T-S		1
T		2
T		3
U1-S		4
U1		5
T-S		6
U1	(5) 6	7
LULL-S		8
U1	9	9
LUUL-S	(5)	10
U1-S		11
LUUL		12
L3-S	5 (6) 7	13
U1	(13)(14)	14
LUUL-S	(9) 10 (11)	15
ULUL	(5) 6 (7)	16
LULL-S		17
U1-S	9 (10)(13)	18
LUUL	(5)	19
T-S		20
U3		21
L3-S	5 (6) 7	22
U1	(13)(14)	23
LUUL-S	(9) 10 (11)	24
ULUL	(5) 6 (7)	25
LULL		26
U1-S	9 (10)(13)	27
U3		28
T		29
LLUL	(5)(7)	30
L3	(9)	31
T	(13)(14)	32
T		33
T		34
T		35
T		36

1		T
2		T
3		T-S
4		U1
5	5	T-S
6		U2-S
7		T
8		LULL-S
9		U3
10	5 (6) 7 (9)(10)	T-S
11		U1
12	(9) 10	LUUL-S
13	(5) 6 (7)	ULUL
14		LULL-S
15	9 (10)(13)	U1-S
16		LUUL
17	5 (6)	T-S
18		U3
19	(9)	LULU-S
20	(5) 6 (7)(13)(14)	U1
21		LULL-S
22	9 (10)	U1
23		LUUL-S
24		U1-S
25	(5) 6 (7)	LUUL
26		L3-S
27	(13)(14)	U1
28	5 (6) 7 (9) 10 (11)	LUUL
29		U3
30	(9)	T
31	(13)	LULL
32	(5)	LLUL
33	(9)(10)	T
34		T
35		T
36		T

Above: 68-bobbin Peruvian fragment design without edge stitches.

Edge Stitches

Edge stitches are coded and made on the edge of the braid in exactly the same way as for 60-bobbin braids. The reversal hand moves to invert the codes are shown below and on the facing page, and in the appendix, pages 172 and 173.

RH & LH Reversal Hand Moves for 68 Bobbin Braids that begin on the Lower Braid

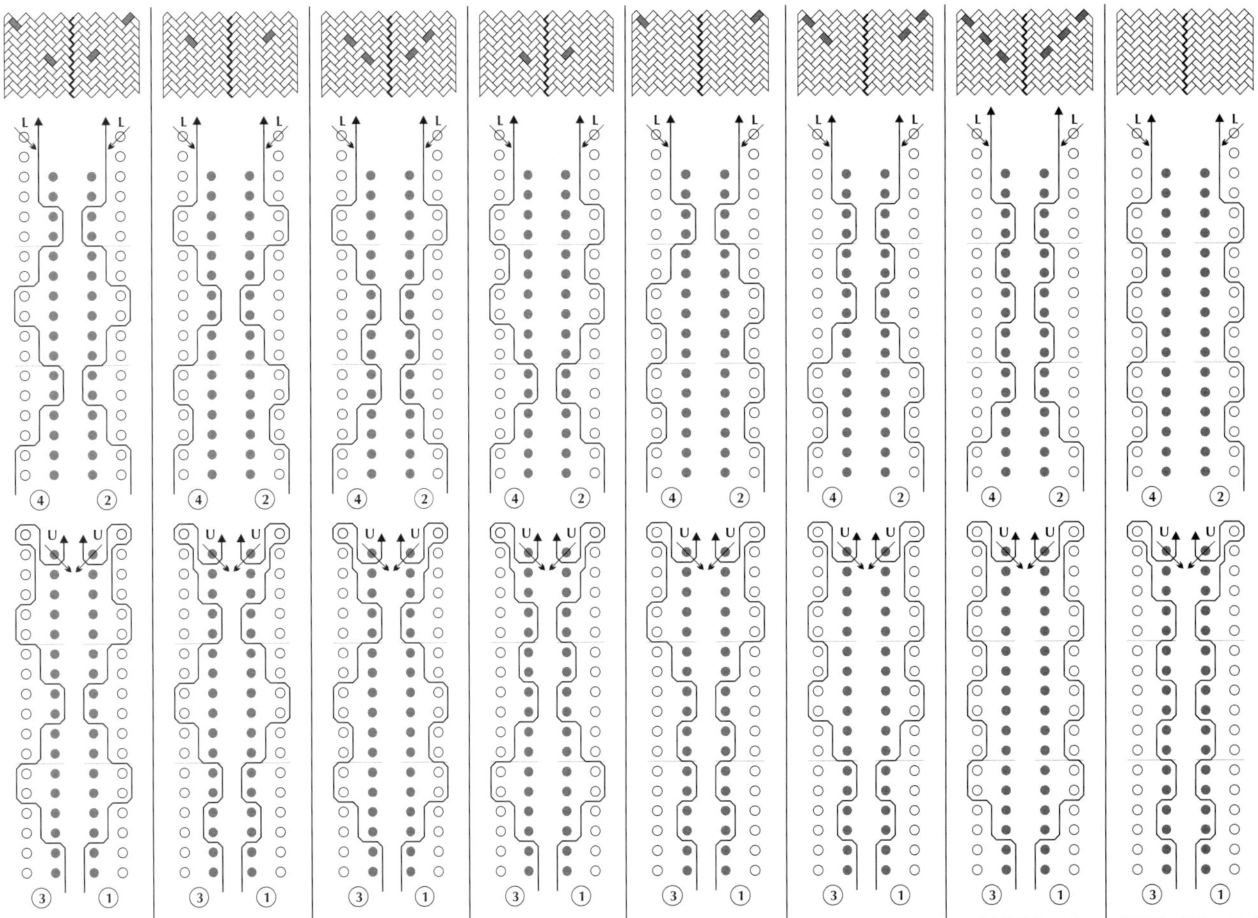

LULU	LLUL	LUUL	LULL	(LLLU)=L3	(LLUU)=L2	(LUUU)=L1	(LLLL)=T for Twill

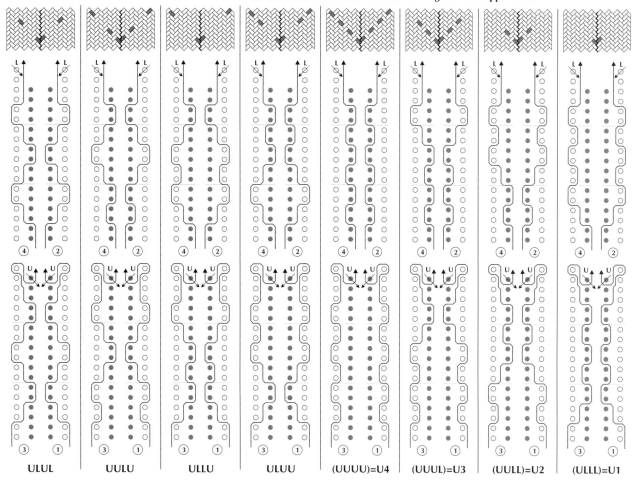

| ULUL | UULU | ULLU | ULUU | (UUUU)=U4 | (UUUL)=U3 | (UULL)=U2 | (ULLL)=U1 |

Small Flames

Weave	Edge	Pick-up	
T-S			1
T-S			2
T-S			3
U1			4
T-S			5
U1-S			6
LULL-S		5 6	7
U2			8
LULL-S			9
ULUL-S		5 (6)(7)	10
LULL-S			11
U3		13	12
LULU		(5)(6) 7	13
L2			14
L3		(9)(10)(13)(14) 15	15
T	LL		16
U4-S	R		17
T	UU		18
T			19
T			20
T			21
T			22
T			23
T			24
T			25

	Pick-up	Edge	Weave
1			T
2			T
3			T
4			ULUL-S
5	9		ULUL-S
6	13		LUUL
7	(5)(6) 7		LUUL
8			ULUU-S
9	(13) 14 15		ULUU-S
10	(5) 6 (7)	LL	LUUL
11		R	ULLU-S
12	13 14 15	R	LULL-S
13	5 (6)(7)	UU	ULUU
14		LL	LUUL
15	13 14(15)	R	ULLU-S
16	(5)(6)(7)	R	U2-S
17		UU	L2
18	13(14)15	LL	LLUL
19		R	UULU-S
20		R	U2-S
21	(13) 14 15	UU	L2
22		LL	LLUL
23		R	UULU-S
24		R	UULU-S
25		UU	T

68-bobbin braid with edge stitches

appendix

Permission is given to photocopy the templates and instructions in the Appendix on the understanding that they are for the reader's own personal use to help plan and make designs.

Under no circumstances are the pages in the Appendix to be printed for re-sale without permission from GMC Publications Ltd.

Contents

A01 and A02 – Are the graph papers for planning single- and twill-braid designs. Instructions on how to use the graph will be found on pages 54–59.

A03 and A04 – 60-bobbin braid graph paper for planning and coding new pick-up designs.

A05 – Master templates from which to cut permanent takatools.

A06 and A07 – 68-bobbin braid graph paper for planning and coding new pick-up designs.

A08 and A09 – 60-bobbin right-hand and left-hand weave-stitch and reversal hand movements.

A10 and A11 – 68-bobbin right-hand and left-hand weave-stitch hand movements.

A12 and A13 – 68-bobbin right-hand and left-hand reversal stitch hand movements.

A14, 15 and 16 – 60-bobbin designs ready for braiding.

A17, 18 and 19 – 68-bobbin designs ready for braiding.

A20 – Record sheet.

A01 *Design graph for single braids*

A02 *Design graph for twill braids*

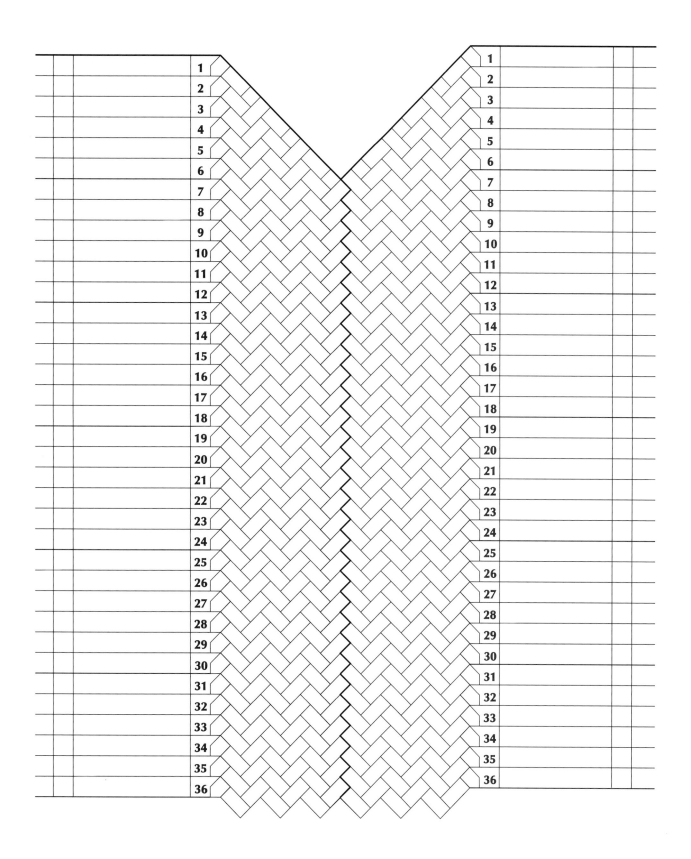

A03 *Twill graph for 60-bobbin pick-up braids*

A04 *Twill graph for 60-bobbin pick-up braids, continuation sheet*

making kumihimo japanese interlaced braids

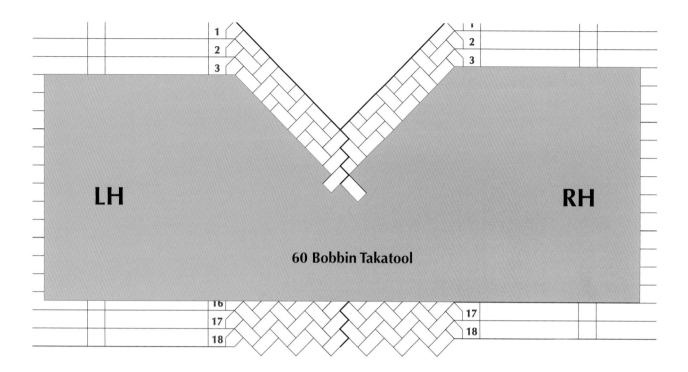

LH

RH

60 Bobbin Takatool

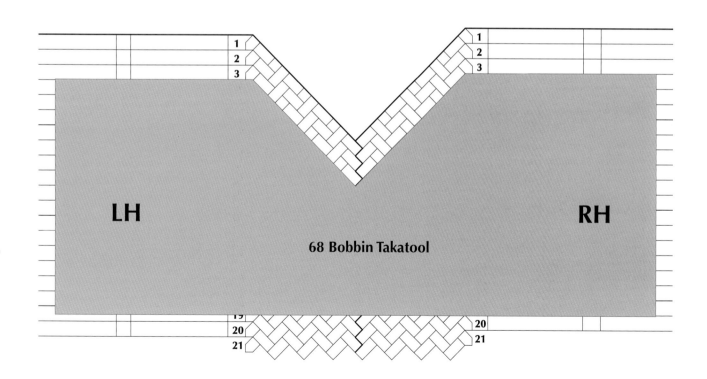

LH

RH

68 Bobbin Takatool

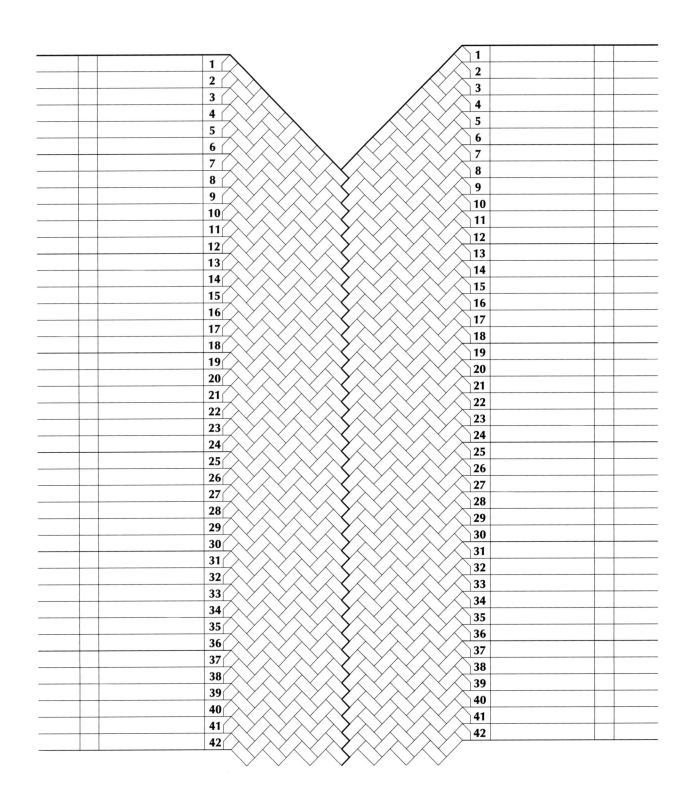

A06 *Twill graph for 68-bobbin pick-up braids*

making kumihimo japanese interlaced braids

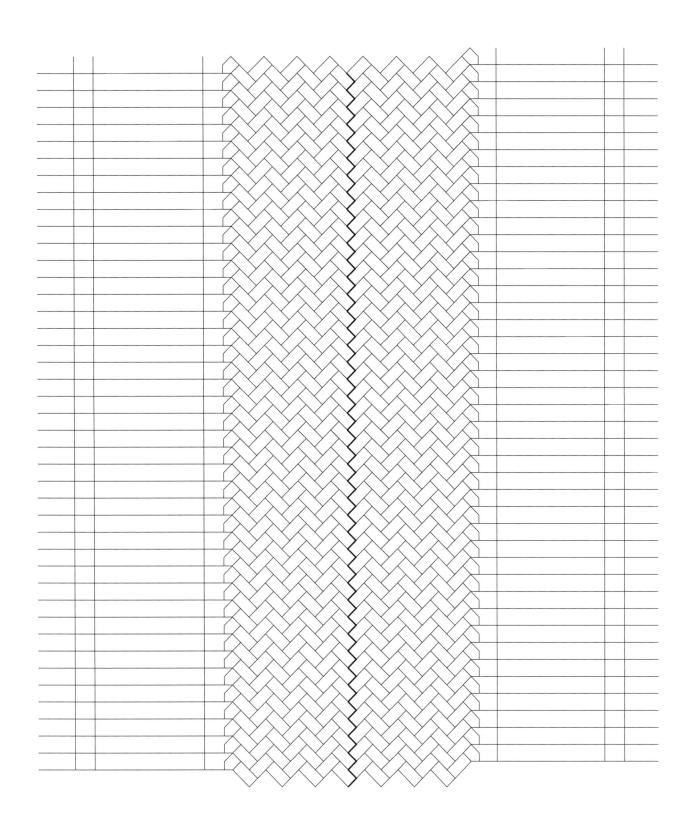

A07 *Twill graph for 68-bobbin pick-up braids, continuation sheet*

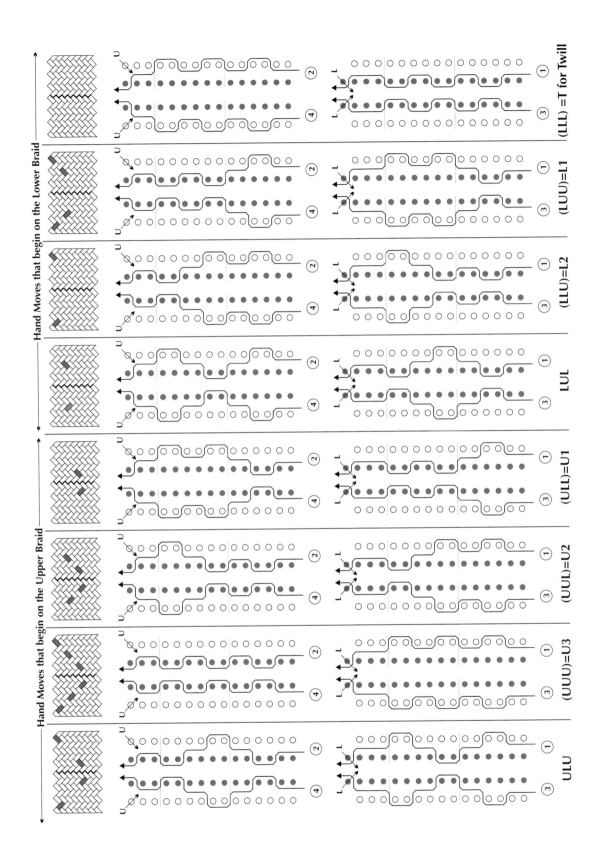

Hand Moves that begin on the Lower Braid

Hand Moves that begin on the Upper Braid

(LLL) =T for Twill
(LUU)=L1
(LLU)=L2
LUL
(ULL)=U1
(UUL)=U2
(UUU)=U3
ULU

A08 *RH & LH weave-stitch hand movements for 60-bobbin braids*

RH & LH Reversal Hand Moves for 60 Bobbin Braids

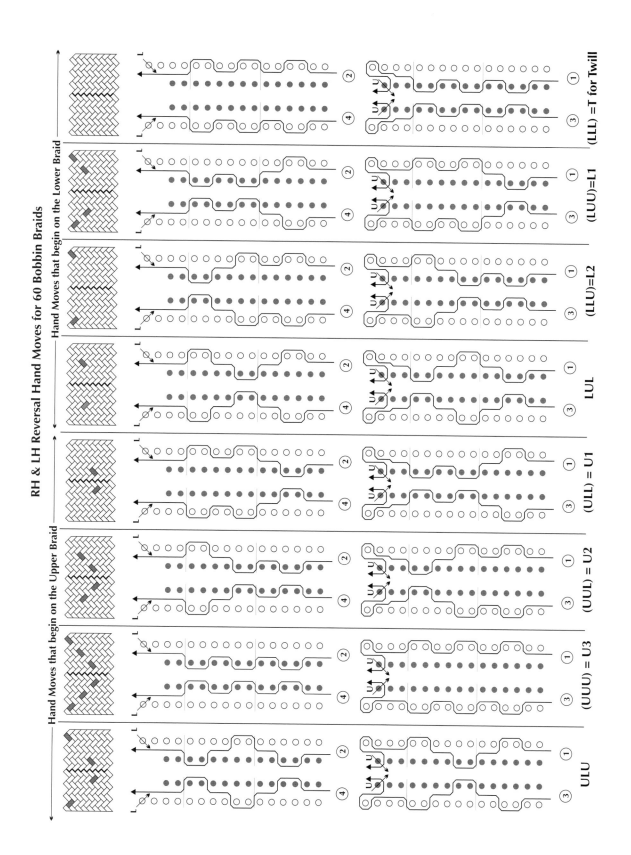

Hand Moves that begin on the Lower Braid

Hand Moves that begin on the Upper Braid

(LLL) =T for Twill

(LUU)=L1

(LLU)=L2

LUL

(ULL) = U1

(UUL) = U2

(UUU) = U3

ULU

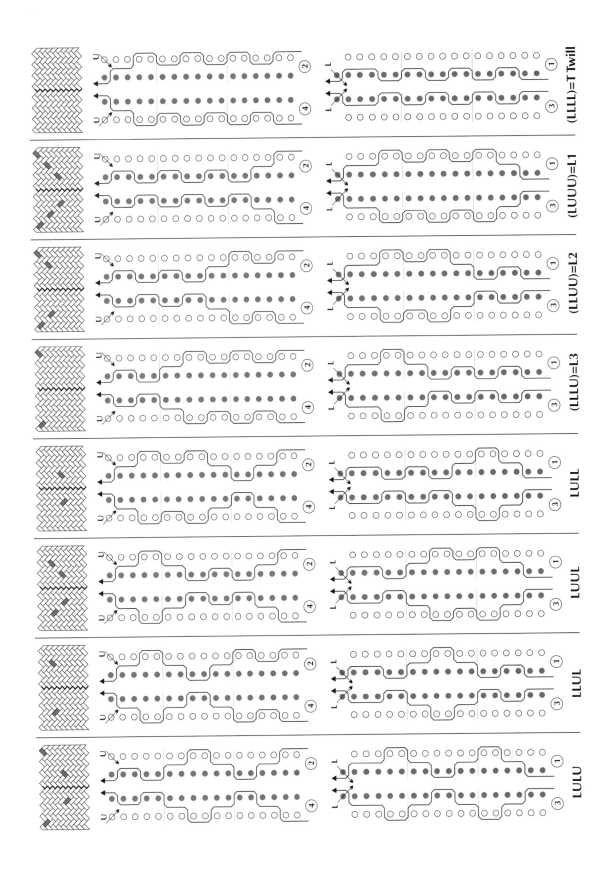

A10 *RH & LH weave-stitch hand moves for 68-bobbin braids that begin on the lower braid*

making kumihimo japanese interlaced braids

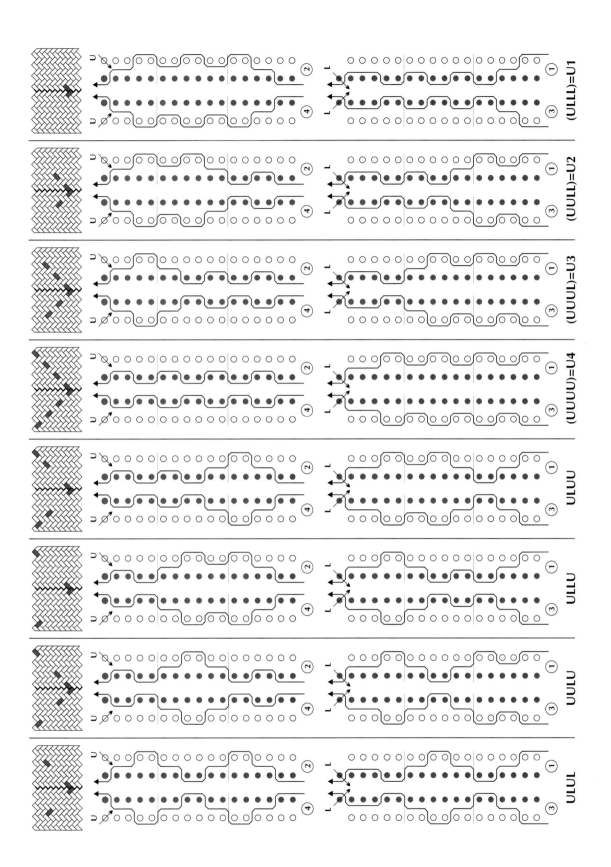

A11 *RH & LH weave stitch hand moves for 68-bobbin braids that begin on the upper braid*

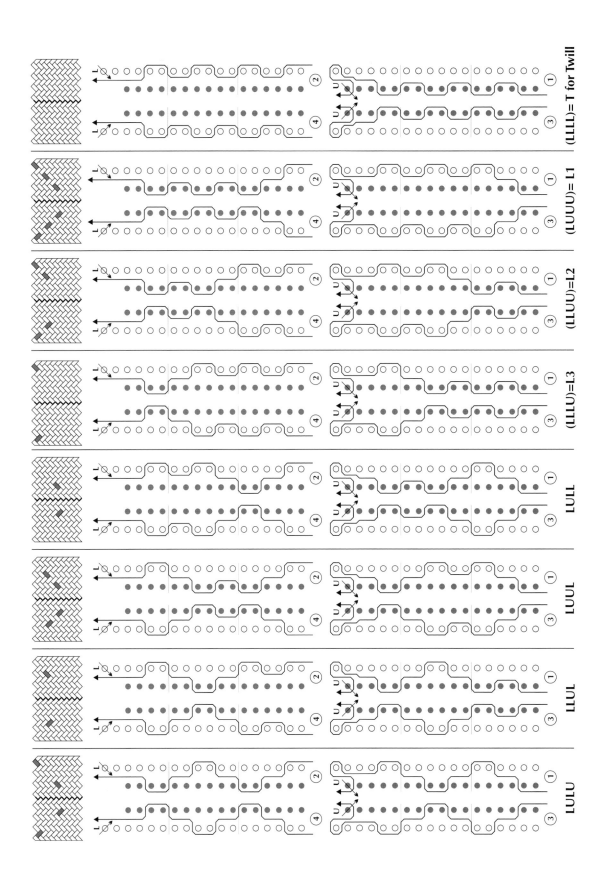

A12 *RH & LH reversal hand moves for 68-bobbin braids that begin on the lower braid*

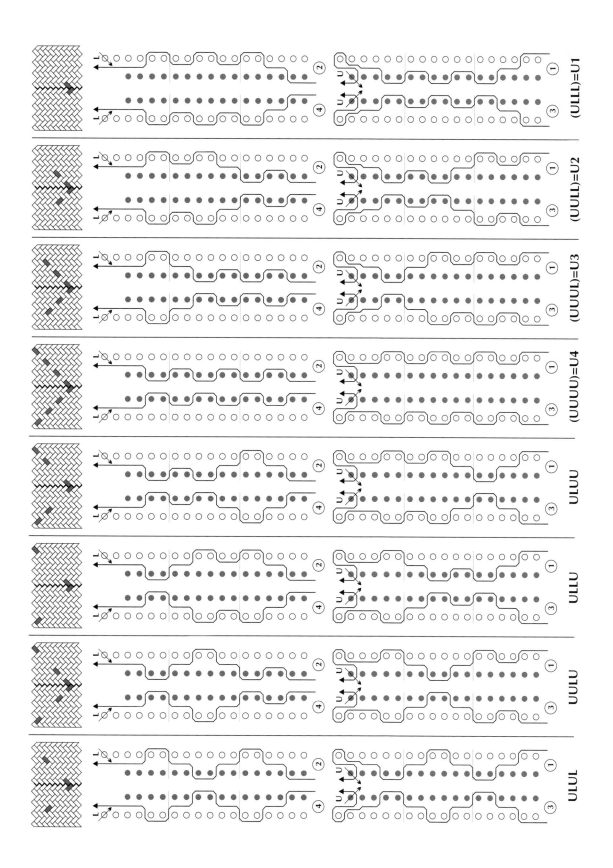

A13 *RH & LH reversal hand moves for 68-bobbin braids that begin on the upper braid*

Move	Numbers	Row
T		1
T		2
T-S		3
T-S		4
U1		5
U1-S	3 4 5	6
T		7
U1-S		8
T		9
U1	3 4 5	10
LUL-S	7 8	11
U1		12
U2-S	3 4 7	13
LUU	11	14
U3		15
LUU-S	3 4 5	16
ULU	7 8	17
LUU-S		18
ULU	7	19
T	11	20
U1-S		21
LUL		22
U1-S	3 4 5 7 9	23
T		24
U1	11	25
LUL-S	3 5	26
T-S	7 9	27
U1	11 12 13	28
U1	3 4 5	29
T		30
T		31
T	3 4 5	32
T		33
T		34
T		35
T		36

Row	Numbers	Move
1		T
2		T-S
3		T-S
4		T-S
5		T-S
6	3	T-S
7		T
8		T-S
9	3 4 5	U1
10		T-S
11	3	U1
12	7	U2-S
13		U2
14	3 4	LUL-S
15		U2
16	3	LUL-S
17	7	T
18		T-S
19	3 4	U1
20		T-S
21	3	U1
22	7	U2-S
23		U2
24	3 4	LUL-S
25		U2-S
26	3	LUL-S
27	7	T-S
28		T-S
29		T-S
30	3 4	T-S
31		T
32		T
33		T
34		T
35		T
36		T

A14 *Spiral design ready for braiding*

A15 *Poppy design ready for braiding*

Left table:

Label	Numbers	Row
T		1
T-S		2
T-S		3
T		4
T-S		5
T-S	(3)	6
T		7
T		8
U1-S	3 4 (5)	9
T-S		10
U2		11
U1	3 (5)(7) 8 9	12
LUL		13
U2		14
L2	3 (11)(12)	15
L1	(7)(8) 9	16
T-S		17
T	3 4 5 (11)(12)	18
T-S	(7)(8)(9)	19
T-S		20
U1	(3)(4)	21
U1-S	(7)(8)(9)	22
T		23
T	(3)(4)	24
T		25
T		26
T		27
T		28
T		29
T		30
T		31
T		32
T		33
T		34
T		35
T		36

Right table:

Row	Numbers	Label
1		T
2		T
3		T
4		U1-S
5	(3) 4 5	T-S
6		U2
7	3 (7) 8 9	U1
8		LUL-S
9		U2-S
10	(11)(12)	L2
11	3 4 (7)(8) 9	L1-S
12		T-S
13	(11)(12)	T
14	(7)(8)(9)	T
15		T
16	3 4 5	T
17	(7)(8)(9)	T
18	3	T-S
19		T-S
20	(7)(8)(9)	U1
21		U1-S
22	(3) 4	LUL-S
23		U2
24		U1
25	(3)(7)(8) 9	U2
26		U2
27	(7)(11)(12)	U1
28		U1
29		U1
30		U1
31		U1
32		T
33		T
34		T
35		T
36		T

			#
T			1
T			2
T			3
T-S			4
T			5
T			6
U1-S		(3) 4	7
U1			8
T-S			9
U1		3 (4) 5 11	10
LUL-S		7 (8) 9	11
ULU			12
LUL-S		3 7	13
U3	LL	11 13	14
L1	UU		15
ULU-S	LL	(3) 4 (5) 7 (8)	16
T-S	R		17
U2	R		18
L1-S	R	3 (4) 5 (7) 8 (9)	19
U1	R	(11) 12 (13)	20
LUL-S	R		21
LUL-S	UU	3 7 9	22
U3	LL	11 13	23
L1	UU		24
L2	LL	(3) (5)	25
U1-S	R	(7) 8 (9)	26
U2-S	R		27
U3-S	R		28
U2-S	R	(11) 12 (13)	29
U3-S	R		30
T	UU		31
T	LL		32
T	UU		33
T			34
T			35
T			36

#			
1			T
2			T
3			T
4			T
5			T-S
6	3 5 11		U1
7	7 9		LUL-S
8			ULU
9	3 7		LUL-S
10	11 13	LL	U3
11		UU	L1
12	(3) 4 (5)	LL	ULU-S
13	(7) 8 (9)	R	T-S
14		R	U2
15	3 (4) 5 (7) 8	R	L1-S
16	(11) 12 (13)	R	U1
17		R	LUL-S
18	3 7 9	UU	LUL-S
19	11 13	LL	U3
20		UU	L1
21	(3) 4 (5)	LL	ULU-S
22	(7) 8 (9)	R	T-S
23		R	U2
24	3 (4) 5	R	L1-S
25	7 (8) 9 (11) 12 (13)	R	U1-S
26		R	LUL-S
27		UU	LUL
28	11 13	LL	L1
29	(7) 9	UU	L1
30		LL	L2
31		R	U2-S
32	(11)	R	U2-S
33		R	U3-S
34		R	U3-S
35		R	U3-S
36		UU	T

A16 *Mountain pass design ready for braiding*

Instruction	Numbers	#
T		1
T		2
T-S		3
U1-S	5 6	4
U2	9 10	5
LUUL-S		6
LUUL-S	(5)(6)	7
LULL	(9)(10) 11	8
U2		9
U2	(13)(14)(15)	10
LULL		11
LULL		12
U2	(5) 7	13
U1	9 10	14
ULUL		15
ULUL	(9)	16
U1		17
T		18
T	(13)(14)(15)	19
T-S		20
U1-S	5 6	21
U2		22
LUUL	9 10 11	23
LLUL	(5)(6)	24
LLUL		25
LLUL	9	26
LLUL	(13)(14)(15)	27
LLUL		28
LLUL	9 10 11	29
LLUL	(13)(14)(15)	30
LLUL		31
T		32
T	(13)(14)(15)	33
T		34
T		35
T		36
		37
		38
		39
		40
		41
		42

#	Numbers	Instruction
1		T
2		T-S
3		T-S
4		T
5		U1
6		U1
7	5	T
8		LULL-S
9		U2-S
10	9	U2
11		LUUL
12	(5)(6)	LLUL
13	(9)(10) 11	T
14	(13)	U1
15		U1
16		U1
17		U1
18		U1
19		T-S
20		T-S
21		T
22		U1
23	9 10 11	ULUL
24		LLUL
25		LUUL
26	(5) 7 9 10 11 (13)(14)	LUUL
27		LLUL
28		LLUL
29	(9) 11 (13)(14)(15)	LLUL
30		T
31		T
32	(13)(14)(15)	T
33		T
34		T
35		T
36		T
37		
38		
39		
40		
41		
42		

A17 *Alpha design ready for braiding*

Left table:

Operation			Row
T-S			1
T			2
U1-S			3
T		5	4
U1-S		9	5
LULL			6
LLUL-S		5	7
T			8
L2-S		9 (10) 11 (13) 14	9
T			10
U4-S		(5)(7)	11
T	LL	(9) 13 15	12
LLUL-S	UU		13
T	LL		14
UULU	R	(5) 7 9 (10) 11	15
L1	R		16
U1	R		17
L1	R		18
L3-S	R	(5)(7)	19
U2-S	UU	(9) 10 (11)(13) 15	20
LUUL	LL		21
LULL-S	R		22
ULLU-S	R		23
L2	UU		24
LULU	LL	(5)(9) 10 13	25
L2	UU		26
T	LL	(9)	27
L3	UU	(13) 14	28
T	LL		29
T	UU		30
T	LL		31
T	UU		32
T			33
T			34
T			35
T			36
			37
			38
			39
			40
			41
			42

Right table:

Row			Operation
1			T
2			T-S
3			U1
4			T-S
5			U1-S
6	(5) 6 9		LULL-S
7			U1-S
8	(5) 13		U3-S
9	(9) 10		UULU
10			LUUL-S
11			ULUU-S
12		LL	LUUL-S
13		UU	ULUU-S
14	(5)(7)	LL	U4
15		UU	UULU-S
16	13 15	LL	LUUL
17		UU	ULUU-S
18		LL	LUUL
19		UU	L2-S
20		LL	L3
21	(5) 7 9 (10) 11	UU	LLUU-S
22	13 15	LL	U1
23		UU	L1
24		LL	T
25	(5) 6 7	UU	LUUL
26	(9) 10 (11)(13) 15	LL	T
27		R	UULU-S
28	(9)	R	U3-S
29	(13)	R	U4-S
30		UU	T
31		LL	T
32		UU	T
33			T
34			T
35			T
36			T
37			
38			
39			
40			
41			
42			

A18 *Fret design ready for braiding*

Left chart:

Label			Row
T			1
T			2
T-S			3
T			4
T			5
U1-S			6
T			7
T			8
U2-S		⑤ 6	9
U1			10
T		5	11
U3-S		⑨ 10	12
U1			13
LULL		5	14
U4-S		⑨ 10 ⑬	15
U1			16
LULL			17
L2-S		⑨ ⑬ 14	18
ULLU			19
LULL		⑬	20
LLUL	LL	⑤	21
L3	UU	⑨	22
T		⑬	23
T			24
T			25
T			26
T			27
T			28
T			29
T			30
T			31
T			32
T			33
T			34
T			35
T			36
			37
			38
			39
			40
			41
			42

Right chart:

Row			Label
1			T
2			T
3			T
4			T
5	5		T-S
6	9		U1
7	13		LULL
8			LLUL-S
9			ULLU
10	5		LULL
11		LL	U3-S
12	13 14	UU	ULLU
13	5		LULL
14	⑨ 10	LL	U3-S
15		R	LUUL-S
16	5	R	ULUU-S
17	⑨ 10 ⑬	R	T
18		UU	L3
19			LULL
20	⑤ 6 ⑨ 10 ⑬	LL	U4
21		UU	L3
22			T
23	⑤ 6 ⑨ 10 ⑪	LL	L1
24		UU	T
25			T
26	⑨ 10 ⑬ 14 15	LL	L2
27		R	U4-S
28		R	U4-S
29	⑬ 14	R	U3-S
30		UU	T
31			T
32		LL	T
33		UU	T
34			T
35			T
36			T
37			
38			
39			
40			
41			
42			

A19 *Arrowhead design ready for braiding*

A20 Takadai Project Sheet

Date ....

Braid description ....

Planned application for braid ....

Fibre – type, size and colour ....

Reason for choice ....

Bobbin weight ....

Setting up method ....

Structure

Plain weave ....Twill 2/2 ....Twill ....3/3 Other ....

Notes on setting up and making ....

Did your design meet your plan? If not, why not, what change will you make? ....

....

Does this suggest other possible designs ....

Costings

Materials

No: Bobbins ....x No: Ends ....x Warp length ....= Total length ....

x £ ($) per yard ....= Material cost ....

Accessories ....= Accessory cost ....

Time taken

Warping ....Setting up ....Making ....= Total time ....

x Hourly rate ....= Labour cost ....

Total cost ....

Finishing off details

Warp length ....
Finished length ....
% shrinkage ....
Excess warp ....
Braid width ....
Pattern pitch ....

suppliers

Key: B = Books E = Equipment Y = Yarns BD = Bodkins C = Clamps

Australia

Artisan Books   B
231 Gertrude Street
Fitzroy, Victoria 3065
Tel: (03) 9416 4805
Fax: (03) 9416 4806
Email:
artisan@alphalink.com.au
Website: www.artisan.com.au

Canada

Ginkgo Associates   E, Y
5 Rothean Drive
Whitby
Ontario L1P 1L5
Tel: 905 666 9720
Email:
104177.1376@compuserve.com

Treenway Silks   Y
501 Musgrave Road
Salt Spring Island
BC V8K 1V5
Tel: 250 653 2345
Fax: 250 653 2347
Email: silk@treenwaysilks.com
Website:
www.treenwaysilks.com

New Zealand

Books Unlimited   B
100 Hone Heke Road
P.O. Box 616
Kerekeri
Tel: (09) 407 7497
Fax: (09) 407 7517
Email:
books.unlimited@xtra.co.nz

Sweden

Jorun Bergström   E, Y
Getfotsvägen 46
122 46 Enskede
Tel: +46 8 649 89 29
Email: info@kumihimo.com
Website: www.kumihimo.com

United Kingdom

Carey Company
B, E, Y
Summercourt
Ridgeway
Ottery St Mary
Devon EX11 1DT
Tel/Fax: 01404 813486
Email:
carey@careycompany.com
Website:
www.careycompany.com

Discount Lighting Ltd   C
The Wherry Quay Boathouse
Bridge Road
Oulton Broad
Suffolk
NR32 2LN
Tel: 01502 587 598
Email:
howard@discountlighting.lt

Edna Gibson   B
70 Furzehatt Road
Plymstock PL9 8QT
Tel: 01752 408262
Email: egibson@globalnet.co.uk

Uppingham Yarns Ltd
Y, BD
22 North Street East
Uppingham LE15 9QL
Tel: 01572 823747
Email: uppyarn@wools.co.uk

United States

Braidershand   B, E, Y
12906 Iscoma Street
San Diego, CA 92129 3613
Tel: 858 484 7807
Email:
service@braidershand.com
Website: www.braidershand.com

Mountain Loom Co   B, E, Y
PO Box 509
Vader, WA 98593 0509
Tel: 360 295 3856
Email:
custserve@mtnloom.com
Website: www.mtnloom.com

A reference guide to all the braids in the book. Numbers shown are the design numbers.

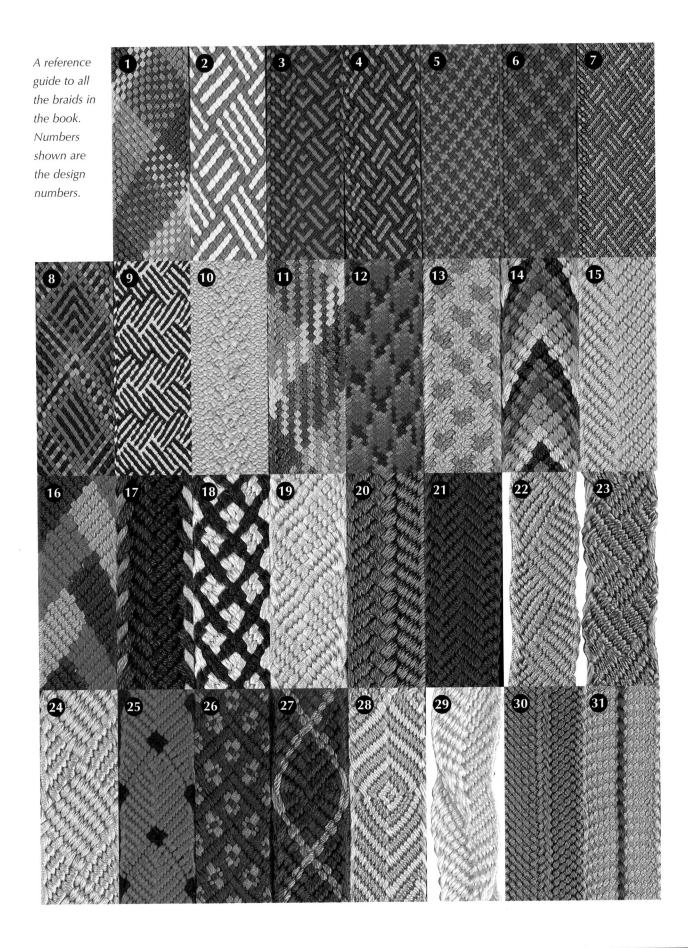

page 174

page 175 page 176 page 177 page 178 page 179 page 142 page 157 page 159

further reading

English Texts

The Mummies of Ürümchi **Elizabeth Wayland Barber** (Norton, 1999)

Samurai Undressed, Carey Company **Jaqui Carey** (The Devonshire Press, 1995)

The Techniques of Ply-Split Braiding **Peter Collingwood** (Bellew Publishing, 1998)

The Basic Book of Finger Weaving **Esther Warner Dendel** (Simon and Schuster, 1974)

'Braiding in Japan' in Celebration of the Curious Mind **Mary Dusenberry** (Interweave Press Inc, 1983)

The Primary Structures of Fabrics **Irene Emery** (The Textile Museum, 1980)

Interlacing, The Elemental Fabric **Jack Lenor Larsen, with Betty Freudenenheim** (Kodansha, 1979)

One/One Plain Weave Twill Braiding in Two Colours **Leigh Morris** (Morris, 2001)

Oblique 2/2 Twill Braids in Two Colours **Leigh Morris** (Morris, 2002)

Braids: 250 Patterns from Japan, Peru & Beyond **Rodrick Owen** (Cassell and Interweave Press, 1995)

Exquisite: The World of Japanese Kumihimo Braiding **Kei Sashi (ed.)** (Kodansha, 1988)

The Art of Japanese Braiding **Noemi Speiser** (CIBA Geigy Review, 1974)

The Manual of Braiding **Noemi Speiser** (Speiser Basel, 1983)

Sixty Sensational Samples from a Decade of Kumihimo Exchanges **Shirley Berlin and Carol Goodwin** (Self-published, 2003)

Japanese with English Texts

The Comprehensive Treatise of Braiding (vols 3 to 5) **Makiko Tada** (Tokyo, 1998–2002)

Hanamusubi, Traditional Flower Knots **Toshiko Tanaka** (Kyoto Shoin Co Ltd, 1993)

Japanese Text

The Works of Tamaki Hirata (vols 1 to 3) **Tamaki Hirata** (Tokyo, 1985–2000)

Kumihimo: An Original Work (Takadai) **Hoetsu Matsushita** (Iga Ueno, 1983)

The Design of Korai Kumihimo (vols 1 to 3) **Miura Yayoi** (Japan, 1986–1990)

Korai Kumihimo, four specialist booklets **Miura Yayoi** (Japan, 1982)

Traditional Kumihimo: Takadai and Taya Takadai **Tomosha Shufno and Itusei Yamaoka** (Domyo, 1976)

Traditional Crafts of Kumihimo **Hoko Tokoro** (Chunichi Newspaper East, 1978)

The Study of Kumihimo **Kaoru Yamamot** (Sogo Gagaku, 1978)

picture credits

Key: **t** top **b** bottom **c** centre **l** left **r** right

5 c Christine Richardson

10 b Rodrick Owen *Chinese collar from the collection of Gwyneth Watkins*

17 c Christine Richardson

18 bl Rodrick Owen *Estonian Woman finger weaving a sash*

19 bl Irene Good at the Peabody Museum *Braids from the Urumchi Mummy Site*;
br Rodrick Owen *Pottery fragment from the Jomon period*

20 bl Rodrick Owen *Replicas of Haniwa figures form the Kofun period*;
br Rodrick Owen *Karakumi braid made by Kazuko Kinoshita*

21 tr Rodrick Owen *Samurai armour, catalogue no. 277548a, Dept. of Anthropology, Smithsonian Institute*; **bl** David Nutt *Saidai-ji temple braid*;
br Rodrick Owen *Samurai sword belt, catalogue no. E095471, Dept. of Anthropology, Smithsonian Institute*

22 br Rodrick Owen *Braided guitar strap*

52 b Rodrick Owen *Braided guitar strap*

61 c Rodrick Owen *A selection of block-pattern braids*

103 b Rodrick Owen *Braided belt made from twill weave with coloured edge*

about the author

Rodrick Owen is a world-respected textile artist and teacher with over 30 years' experience. As a commissioned artist his clients include Sir Paul McCartney and textile designers, as well as commissions for industry. His designs have been published in numerous books and magazines, and he is the author of a previous book, *Braids: 250 Patterns form Japan, Peru and Beyond*.

Rodrick specializes in traditional forms of braid making and, in 1984, was awarded a Winston Churchill Fellowship to study Kumihimo in Japan, where he was also invited to teach at two universities in Tokyo. Subsequently, his work has been exhibited worldwide, and he has continued to teach in the USA, Europe and Australia.

acknowledgements

In England I would thank Braid Society members Christine Ablett, Edna Gibson, Sandy Jessett and Jan Rawdon-Smith for reading and working the original instructions, and for their suggestions that set this project on course. To Len and Daphne Crisp who developed and made the takadai, for without their woodworking skills there would have been no equipment on which to make these braids. My special thanks to Jennie Parry who has supported me over the years by challenging my thinking, sharing her detailed knowledge and allowing me to use many of her photographs. I would also thank the Joan Howes Trust and Southern Arts.

In America my special thanks goes to three people whose continued enthusiasm and commitment that have helped the final shape of the book. To Terry Flynn, who in 1994 seeded the idea that I write a monograph on the takadai, and who through a series of teaching programmes arranged at *The Weaver's Place* in Baltimore allowed me to develop the material for the book. For sharing her creative ideas of how to use braids as fabric for scarves and garments, and for showing me the correlation between weaving and interlaced braids.

To Richard Sutherland, who reviewed the text to present the language in a less technical way for people new to interlaced braids, for bridging the transatlantic language differences, and for testing the designs and making braid samples. And finally to Duane Wakeham for his background work, the calming energy and for being there – thank you, Cook. My thanks also to Jackie Wollenberg and all the students at the *Hen House* in Fort Bragg, California, who gather annually to make braids.

I would thank the many fibre people worldwide who have shown me textile samples and who have shared their photographs and information, and the many museums that have allowed me access to their collections and permission to photograph. In particular I would thank Dr Irene Good for allowing me to use her photographs of the braids from the Ürümchi burial site.

Lastly, my thanks to Tamaki Hirata, Yayoi Miura and Makiko Tada – esteemed Japanese braiding artists whose skills have inspired me to write and share this unique traditional Japanese art form.

Domo Arigato-gozimashita

index

CRAFTS

Bargello: A Fresh Approach to Florentine Embroidery *Brenda Day*

Bead and Sequin Embroidery Stitches *Stanley Levy*

Beginning Picture Marquetry *Lawrence Threadgold*

Blackwork: A New Approach *Brenda Day*

Celtic Backstitch *Helen Hall*

Celtic Cross Stitch Designs *Carol Phillipson*

Celtic Knotwork Designs *Sheila Sturrock*

Celtic Knotwork Handbook *Sheila Sturrock*

Celtic Spirals and Other Designs *Sheila Sturrock*

Celtic Spirals Handbook *Sheila Sturrock*

Complete Pyrography *Stephen Poole*

Creating Made-to-Measure Knitwear: A Revolutionary Approach to Knitwear Design *Sylvia Wynn*

Creative Backstitch *Helen Hall*

Creative Log-Cabin Patchwork *Pauline Brown*

Creative Machine Knitting *GMC Publications*

Cross-Stitch Designs from China *Carol Phillipson*

Cross-Stitch Designs from India *Carol Phillipson*

Cross-Stitch Floral Designs *Joanne Sanderson*

Cross-Stitch Gardening Projects *Joanne Sanderson*

Decoration on Fabric: A Sourcebook of Ideas *Pauline Brown*

Decorative Beaded Purses *Enid Taylor*

Designing and Making Cards *Glennis Gilruth*

Designs for Pyrography and Other Crafts *Norma Gregory*

Dried Flowers: A Complete Guide *Lindy Bird*

Easy Wedding Planner *Jenny Hopkin*

Exotic Textiles in Needlepoint *Stella Knight*

Glass Engraving Pattern Book *John Everett*

Glass Painting *Emma Sedman*

Handcrafted Rugs *Sandra Hardy*

Hobby Ceramics: Techniques and Projects for Beginners *Patricia A. Waller*

How to Arrange Flowers: A Japanese Approach to English Design *Taeko Marvelly*

How to Make First-Class Cards *Debbie Brown*

An Introduction to Crewel Embroidery *Mave Glenny*

Machine-Knitted Babywear *Christine Eames*

Making Fabergé-Style Eggs *Denise Hopper*

Making Fairies and Fantastical Creatures *Julie Sharp*

Making Hand-Sewn Boxes: Techniques and Projects *Jackie Woolsey*

Making Kumihimo: Japanese Interlaced Braids *Rodrick Owen*

Making Mini Cards, Gift Tags & Invitations *Glennis Gilruth*

Making Wirecraft Cards *Kate MacFadyen*

Native American Bead Weaving *Lynne Garner*

New Ideas for Crochet: Stylish Projects for the Home *Darsha Capaldi*

Paddington Bear in Cross-Stitch *Leslie Hills*

Papercraft Projects for Special Occasion *Sine Chesterman*

Papermaking and Bookbinding: Coastal Inspirations *Joanne Kaar*

Patchwork for Beginners *Pauline Brown*

Pyrography Designs *Norma Gregory*

Rose Windows for Quilters *Angela Besley*

Silk Painting for Beginners *Jill Clay*

Sponge Painting *Ann Rooney*

Stained Glass: Techniques and Projects *Mary Shanahan*

Step-by-Step Pyrography Projects for the Solid Point Machine *Norma Gregory*

Stitched Cards and Gift Tags for Special Occasions *Carol Phillipson*

Tassel Making for Beginners *Enid Taylor*

Tatting Collage *Lindsay Rogers*

Tatting Patterns *Lyn Morton*

Temari: A Traditional Japanese Embroidery Technique *Margaret Ludlow*

Three-Dimensional Découpage: Innovative Projects for Beginners *Hilda Stokes*

Trompe l'Oeil: Techniques and Projects *Jan Lee Johnson*

Tudor Treasures to Embroider *Pamela Warner*

Wax Art *Hazel Marsh*

WOODCARVING

Beginning Woodcarving *GMC Publications*

Carving Architectural Detail in Wood: The Classical Tradition *Frederick Wilbur*

Carving Birds & Beasts *GMC Publications*

Carving Classical Styles in Wood *Frederick Wilbur*

Carving the Human Figure: Studies in Wood and Stone *Dick Onians*

Carving Nature: Wildlife Studies in Wood *Frank Fox-Wilson*

Celtic Carved Lovespoons: 30 Patterns *Sharon Littley & Clive Griffin*

Decorative Woodcarving (New Edition) *Jeremy Williams*

Elements of Woodcarving *Chris Pye*

Figure Carving in Wood: Human and Animal Forms *Sara Wilkinson*

Lettercarving in Wood: A Practical Course *Chris Pye*

Relief Carving in Wood: A Practical Introduction *Chris Pye*

Woodcarving for Beginners *GMC Publications*

Woodcarving Made Easy *Cynthia Rogers*

Woodcarving Tools, Materials & Equipment (New Edition in 2 vols.) *Chris Pye*

WOODTURNING

Bowl Turning Techniques Masterclass *Tony Boase*

Chris Child's Projects for Woodturners *Chris Child*

Decorating Turned Wood: The Maker's Eye *Liz & Michael O'Donnell*

Green Woodwork *Mike Abbott*